SPEED READ

C000104546

Inspiring | Educating | Creating | Entertaining

Brimming with creative inspiration, how-to projects, and useful information to enrich your everyday life, Quarto Knows is a favorite destination for those pursuing their interests and passions. Visit our site and dig deeper with our books into your area of interest: Quarto Creates, Quarto Cooks, Quarto Homes, Quarto Lives, Quarto Drives, Quarto Explores, Quarto Gifts, or Quarto Kids.

© 2017 Quarto Publishing Group USA Inc.

First Published in 2017 by Motorbooks, an imprint of The Quarto Group,
100 Cummings Center, Suite 265-D, Beverly, MA 01915, USA.
T (978) 282-9590 F (978) 283-2742 QuartoKnows.com

All rights reserved. No part of this book may be reproduced in any form without written permission of the copyright owners. All images in this book have been reproduced with the knowledge and prior consent of the artists concerned, and no responsibility is accepted by producer, publisher, or printer for any infringement of copyright or otherwise, arising from the contents of this publication. Every effort has been made to ensure that credits accurately comply with information supplied. We apologize for any inaccuracies that may have occurred and will resolve inaccurate or missing information in a subsequent reprinting of the book.

Motorbooks titles are also available at discount for retail, wholesale, promotional, and bulk purchase. For details, contact the Special Sales Manager by email at specialsales@quarto.com or by mail at The Quarto Group, Attn: Special Sales Manager, 100 Cummings Center, Suite 265-D, Beverly, MA 01915, USA.

10 9 8 7 6 5 4 3 2

ISBN: 978-0-7603-5562-6

Library of Congress Control Number: 2017946396

Acquiring Editor: Darwin Holmstrom
Project Manager: Jordan Wiklund
Series Creative Director: Laura Drew
Cover and interior design: Laura Drew
Cover illustrations by Chris Rathbone
Interior illustrations by Chris Rathbone except where noted below.
Illustrations © Shutterstock: 2, 7, 8, 9, 24, 25, 26, 27, 40, 41, 42, 43, 82, 83, 84, 85, 98, 99, 100, 101, 116, 117, 118, 119, 136, 137, 138, 139, 154, 155

Printed in China

SPEED READ

F1

THE TECHNOLOGY, RULES, HISTORY AND CONCEPTS KEY TO THE SPORT

STUART CODLING

F1

INTRODUCTION
IT ALL STARTS WITH A NAME: FORMULA 1

But where did that name come from?

The world racing championship that now encompasses twenty (and counting) annual races across five continents was originally defined by the type of car allowed to compete.

Formula 1 (F1) racing as we know it today started in the European racing scene between the first and second world wars. In that interwar period, the races served to showcase some of the biggest manufacturers of the day, featuring the fastest and most powerful prototype machinery.

World War II put racing on a temporary hiatus. When that conflict ended, motorsport's governing body tentatively set out a number of categories—formulae—based on the cars already in existence. This meant that many of the first F1 cars had been around since the late 1930s and had somehow escaped being melted down for munitions during the war.

The world championship for drivers began in 1950, followed by one for manufacturers in 1958. In the decades that followed, the sport has changed almost beyond recognition. The races have become slightly shorter, the cars massively more complex, and the rules more prescriptive and tightly enforced. No aspect of the sport's operation has escaped the reach of commercial thinking.

When Britain's King George VI watched the field roar away at the first World Championship Formula 1 Race at Silverstone in May 1950, gasoline was still rationed in his dominion and the circuit itself was a redundant airfield bounded by old oil drums. Today, contemporary Grands Prix are tightly choreographed television spectacles, set in multimillion-dollar facilities, and waving the flag for some of the world's most prestigious brands.

The years between the first Grand Prix and today's events brought growing pains, controversies, civil wars, glory, and, sadly, death. When the starting lights go out on a Grand Prix Sunday, every part of the spectacle has been shaped by lessons learned—often the hard way—over seven decades of rip-roaring action.

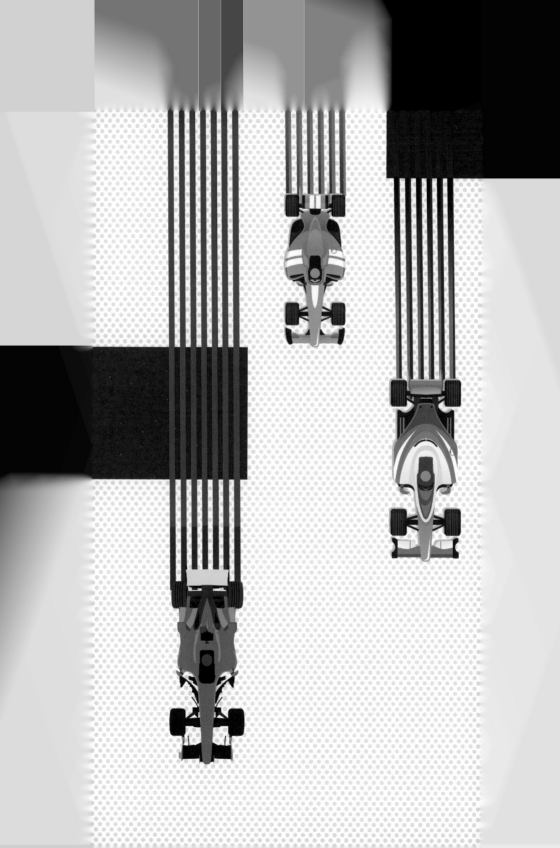

TECHNOLOGY

FUN FACT

The fastest-revving F1 engine in history was the Cosworth CA2006, a 2.4-liter V-8 that exceeded 20,000 rpm. Since 2014, engines have been limited to 15,000 rpm.

HISTORICAL TIDBIT

The British team BRM were responsible for two of the strangest engines in F1 history, a 1.5-liter supercharged V-16 and a 3-liter H-16 (essentially two V-8 blocks, flattened and joined). Neither were very successful but they made a great noise.

KEY PERSON

UK driver Andy Cowell is the chief of Mercedes-Benz High Performance Powertrains, whose power unit has been the performance benchmark throughout the hybrid turbo era.

Formula 1 engines today put their road car cousins to shame in terms of fuel efficiency—while still squeezing around 1,000 horsepower from 1.6-liter V-6s. Manufacturers prefer the term "power unit," since the total horsepower output is a cooperative effort between the turbocharged internal combustion engine and a cutting-edge hybrid system.

When a turbocharger expels heat, that energy can be recovered, stored, and deployed at will, either to provide an instant power kick or to eliminate turbo lag, one of the main disadvantages of turbocharging. A turbo works by using exhaust gases to drive a pump, compressing the air that goes into the engine. While the turbo spins up, there is a natural delay between pressing the accelerator and getting the power boost. An F1 car's hybrid system uses recovered heat energy to keep the turbo spinning, so the boost is always ready.

To keep technology focused on efficiency, F1 rules enforce a strict limit on the amount of fuel carried by cars (105 kilograms) and how fast it can flow (100 kilograms/hour). Since 2010, no refueling has been allowed during races.

F1 engines have changed a great deal since the world championship began in 1950, when 1.5-liter supercharged or 4.5-liter naturally aspirated engines of any cylinder count were permitted. For most of that time, engines were ear-splittingly loud; today, though, race cars' physically smaller engines are restricted to 15,000 rpm and breathe through turbochargers, with the side effect of muffling the exhaust sound.

To reduce costs, engine development is restricted. Beginning with the 2017 season, teams are limited to four complete power units per driver per season. Once a driver burns through the quota of components, he or she begins to incur increasingly severe grid penalties. This gives the manufacturers a major incentive to focus on reliability as well as power and economy.

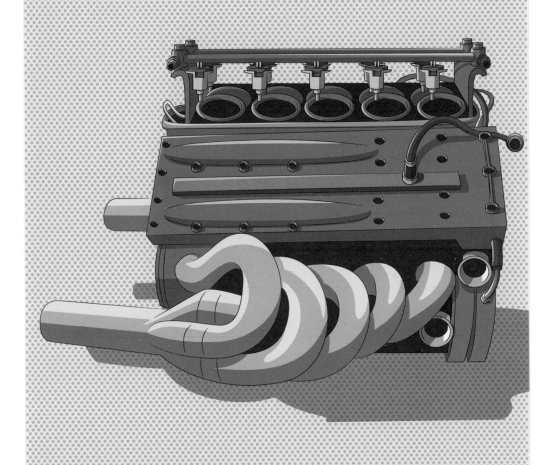

FUN FACT

Carbon fiber is a flexible woven material that arrives in a roll, like carpet. It's cut into pieces of specific size and shape, layered in a mold with resin, and finally vacuum-sealed and baked at high pressure.

HISTORICAL TIDBIT

The first McLaren Formula 1 car was built of an unusual composite material, Mallite, which is made of balsawood sheets lined with duralumin, an early type of aluminum alloy. Though lighter than steel, it was difficult to work into curved shapes.

KEY PERSON

Lotus founder Colin Chapman was obsessed with weight: he famously described his design mantra as "added lightness." His chassis innovations were often copied in the 1960s and 1970s.

If the engine is the heart of a Formula 1 car, the chassis is its spine. Every element connects to the chassis and relies on its strength.

In the early days of the World Championship, chassis were typically built as a steel frame. This could take the form of a flat perimeter design that looked like a ladder, or the frame could appear as a more sophisticated, three-dimensional network of tubing known as a space frame. The engine, gearbox, suspension, and outer body panels were then mounted on the frame, usually with the engine in front of the driver.

During the late 1950s and early 1960s, three key changes transformed the sport. First, the Cooper team started winning races—and then championships—with cars whose engines were mounted behind the driver, giving a better handling balance.

Then another team, Lotus, introduced a car whose outer skin was designed as an integral, load-bearing part of the chassis rather than just being dead weight. This evolved into using the engine as part of the car's structure, a change that Ford underwrote in its development of a new V-8 in 1966.

Manufacturers built chassis from steel and aluminum until 1981, when McLaren shocked the F1 world with the MP4, which featured a carbon-fiber chassis. Carbon fiber quickly became the chassis material of choice, and remains so to this day.

A modern F1 car is built around a central carbon-fiber structure called a "tub," which includes the cockpit. These tubs have to pass a series of static load and crash tests, including a simulated rollover. The cockpit wall, for example, must withstand an impact equivalent to 250 tons.

To keep the competition as fair as possible throughout a Grand Prix weekend, the cars must weigh at least 728 kilograms, including the driver but not the fuel. Each car's weight is checked at random during the weekend and again immediately after the race.

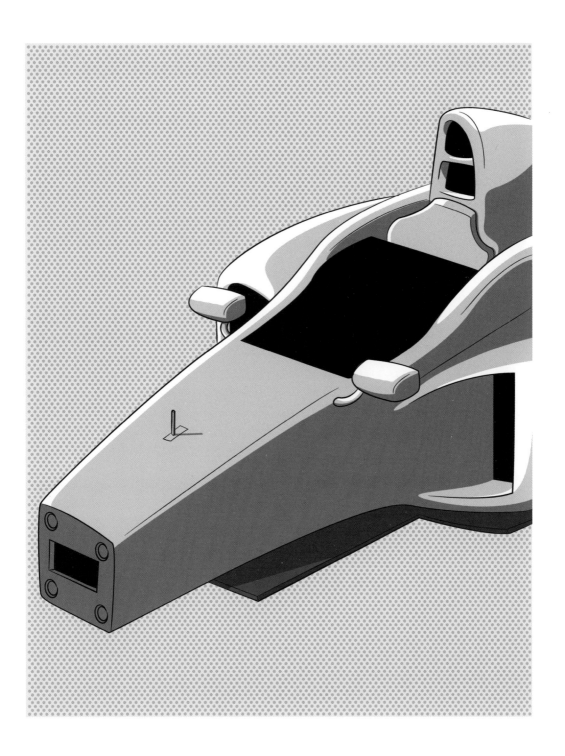

TECHNOLOGY
ELECTRONICS

FUN FACT

The standardized engine control unit (ECU), currently the TAG-320, also controls the radio and the driver's drinking bottle.

HISTORICAL TIDBIT

In 1994, the Benetton team's laptop computers were confiscated and analyzed by F1's governing body. They discovered a hidden menu—"Option 13"—in the software, which gave access to illegal traction control functions. The team was caught, but they couldn't be punished: the officials couldn't prove it had been used.

KEY PERSON

Tad Czapski was a key figure with Benetton, Ferrari, and Renault in the 1990s and early 2000s. He's credited with pushing forward the science of engine control software.

The days of the engine and gearbox being physically connected to the throttle pedal and gearshift are long gone. A typical Formula 1 car racing today contains almost a kilometer of wiring, and sophisticated electronic systems govern and monitor all aspects of its performance.

Even the brakes have an element of electronic control, if only at the rear, to mitigate the effects of the energy recovery system (ERS). The problem occurs when the ERS adds to the braking force on the rear wheels as they harvest energy, potentially giving the driver a nasty surprise if peak charge is reached and the brakes shut off in a braking zone. The electronics help by interpreting the amount of braking force the driver wants, based on how hard the pedal has been depressed, and then adjusting the hydraulic pressure to the rear brake calipers if the ERS effect changes.

Apart from this, electronic systems designed to help the driver—such as anti-lock brakes or traction control—are forbidden. This ban is effectively policed by the presence of a standard electronic "hub" common to all cars; currently, the hub used for F1 racing is the TAG-320, supplied by McLaren Applied Technologies.

Electronics also play a crucial role in boosting performance and avoiding or diagnosing breakdowns. Every movement of a Formula 1 car is monitored by a network of sensors and transmitted back to the team—usually in real time. The data they capture—up to half a megabyte per second—can help both car and driver perform better, as well as giving early warning of technical failures.

Since there are just under 100 sensors within the car, by the end of each track session the team has a vast quantity of information to sift through. They can use it to work out whether the changes they've made have had an effect and how much the performance of individual elements such as the tires change over time. They can also analyze the driver's inputs into the controls to decide if they're leaving time on the table.

That, as you can imagine, sometimes makes for a tricky conversation.

TECHNOLOGY
AERODYNAMICS

FUN FACT

A Formula 1 car's wings produce so much downforce at racing speed that the vehicle could run upside down on a ceiling—provided you found one that was long enough.

HISTORICAL TIDBIT

"Ground effect"—sealing off the car's underbody to create a low-pressure area that sucks it to the ground and boosts its cornering speed—came to F1 by accident. Lotus aerodynamicist Peter Wright was working in the wind tunnel when the center of the model began to sag.

KEY PERSON

Adrian Newey is considered the finest aerodynamicist of his generation in Formula 1. Cars designed on his watch have won ten drivers' championships in the past twenty-five years.

It's the tangle of conflicting needs that makes aerodynamics such an important and controversial area in the world of Formula 1. At its heart is the tradeoff between straight-line speed and cornering performance: designers spend hundreds of hours researching parts that help their cars go around corners quicker, but they can also slow the cars down when travelling in a straight line.

Any object moving through air or fluid encounters resistance, known as drag. In the early days of Formula 1, designers focused on making the cars slim and narrow, and on keeping elements such as suspension components out of the airflow. The key to speed, they believed, was to present the minimum possible surface area to the air through which the car was passing.

This changed in the 1960s, as radical thinkers realized that, by following the principles of flight in reverse—adding wings to generate downward thrust rather than lift—they could go beyond the natural grip levels of the tires and make their vehicles go faster around corners. The wings added drag, which cost top speed, but overall lap times were quicker.

After this, the race was on to get the best of both worlds: maximum speed in a straight line *and* around corners.

Modern F1 cars have large wings front and rear, but they also feature many smaller elements intended to create vortices that can speed up the air as it passes over the car. Since the wheels and tires are a major air blockage, parts of the front wing are designed to steer air away from the wheels.

Aerodynamic research is conducted both in the wind tunnel, with physical models, and virtually, via computational fluid dynamics (CFD). As teams began to spend ever greater sums in the "aero arms race" of the early 2000s, the sport's governing body responded by clamping down. Wind tunnel hours and computing power are now subject to strict limits.

FUN FACT

After a crash or breakdown, cars have to be left in neutral and with the steering wheel fitted so it can be removed easily. At Monaco in 2010 Rubens Barrichello was lucky to get away with tossing his steering wheel onto the track... where it was hit by another car.

HISTORICAL TIDBIT

Andrea de Cesaris demonstrated the importance of keeping both hands on the steering wheel at Long Beach in 1982. He was leading the race for Alfa Romeo until he shook his fist at an uncooperative backmarker and missed a gearchange.

KEY PERSON

British designer John Barnard pioneered the paddle-shift semi-automatic gearchange system in the 1989 Ferrari 640. Until then, all F1 cars used a stick shift.

Except for the accelerator and brakes, everything Formula 1 drivers need for control is now available at their fingertips. Over the sixty-plus years of the World Championship, steering wheels have evolved from simple wood-rimmed tillers to painstakingly designed and custom-built pieces of carbon-fiber art. Paddle switches behind the wheel control the clutch and gearshift, so the driver never has to take his or her hands off the wheel.

The sheer number of switches, dials, and buttons (between thirty and forty, depending on driver preference) is a window on the incredibly complex inner life of a modern F1 car. On-the-fly changes to performance are required from corner to corner, and today's F1 cars are designed to handle them.

Dials in the center of the wheel can fine-tune the differential settings and engine-torque delivery as needed, adjusting the car's behavior in particular corners or with changing track conditions. The driver can also alter the ignition mapping and fuel-air mix, depending on whether he or she needs more power or fuel economy. Other rotary switches enable the driver to move the balance of braking force from front or rear, or to change the priorities of the power unit's energy recovery and storage systems.

To cut down on clutter, most teams map the systems that need to be adjusted less often (such as the rev limiter) to one multi-function rotary dial, usually placed in the center of the wheel.

Buttons control instant-hit functions such as the drinking bottle, the radio, the pit lane speed limiter, and the drag-reduction system activator. There's also a separate button (usually marked "ACK") for when the driver is too busy to talk but needs to acknowledge a message from the pit wall. He also has a button (usually marked "BOX") for telling the team that he's coming in to the pits.

In 2014, a 480 x 272-pixel color LCD screen was introduced along with the new hybrid power unit formula, though some teams have retained the old monochrome screen.

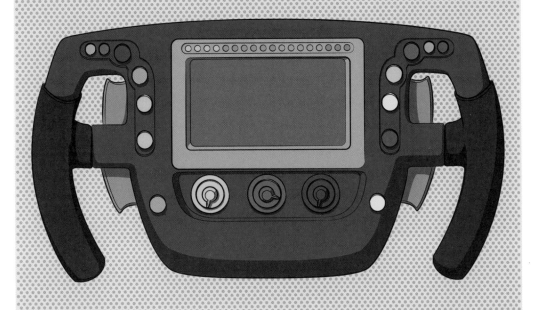

TECHNOLOGY
FUEL AND LUBES

FUN FACT

The Force India team has pet names for the two fuel-dispensing machines it keeps in its garage: Bert and Ernie, after the *Sesame Street* characters.

HISTORICAL TIDBIT

One of F1's most persistent myths is that Nelson Piquet's 1983 championship-winning Brabham BMW was powered by a special fuel, first developed in Nazi Germany to power V2 rockets. This theory has been discredited, but it still pops up on blogs and web forums.

KEY PERSON

Enzo Ferrari was one of the first team bosses to form a long-term relationship with a fuel supplier. After 1950, his team worked exclusively with Shell.

The scene of racing drivers thanking their sponsors and suppliers after a successful race is a familiar sight. It may seem like an exercise in box-checking, but, in the case of the fuel and lubes suppliers, those thanks are well deserved.

The rules for fuel use became one of the first open conflicts in Formula 1, as competitors loaded up with power-boosting additives. In the postwar years, fuel was often inconsistent in quality and difficult to obtain (the first World Championship race was held in Britain in May 1950, when fuel was still rationed there). What went in the tank was more likely to be a toxic cocktail of aviation fuel, benzene, and alcohol than petrol.

As with many other areas of the competition, the governing body gradually tightened up the rules. Aviation gas was banned in the 1950s, and for a while only pump fuel was allowed.

Current F1 fuel is close to what you can buy at a gas station, although leading teams and engine manufacturers work with their fuel and lubes suppliers to create a family of blends to suit different circuits and climates. Each of these has to be submitted to the governing body for tests, where the fluids' chemical "fingerprints" are taken. Regular checks are also conducted at races to ensure competitors aren't using special fuel.

As well as boosting engine power and reducing losses through friction, fuel and lubes can also help with aerodynamic performance. Less friction means less heat, allowing cars to run with smaller radiator air intakes—another way to reduce drag.

Some suppliers bring mobile testing laboratories with them to races. These allow for on-the-spot health checks to test oil samples for the presence of metal and other contaminants, all indicators of excess wear or imminent failure.

Under current regulations, Formula 1 cars can use no more than 105 kilograms of fuel during a race.

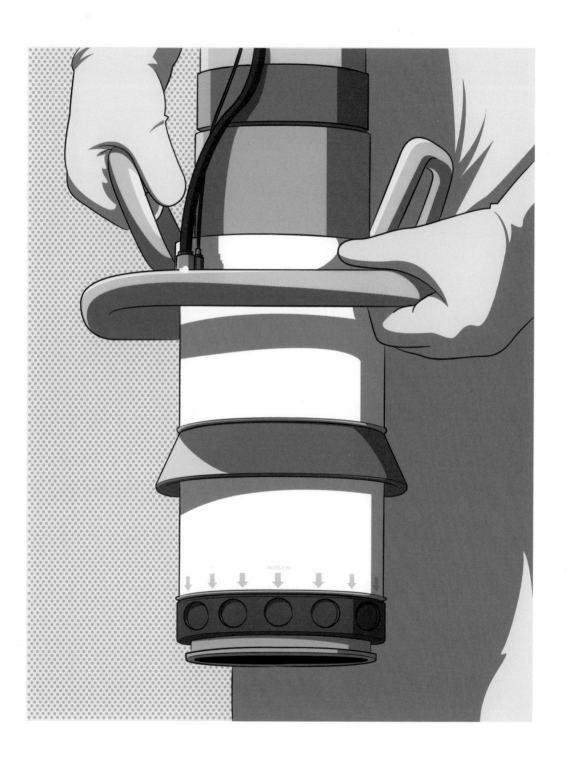

BANNED!

Formula 1 represents the pinnacle of motor racing technology, but sometimes engineers overreach and design systems that have to be put back in the box. Complaints about such tech usually originate with rival teams who have failed to copy it effectively themselves.

ACTIVE SUSPENSION

Pioneered in the early 1980s but then dropped because the control systems were heavy, primitive, and unreliable, active suspension became a game-changer when the Williams team perfected it in 1992. Computer-controlled hydraulic systems interlinked all four corners of the car, keeping it flat relative to the track surface. This enabled the team to run a very aggressive aerodynamic setup that would otherwise be compromised by normal car movements, such as pitch and roll.

FIDDLE BRAKE

Under heavy loads, the brake discs on an F1 car can reach 1,000 degrees Celsius, so it's not unusual to see them glowing, even in daylight. In the late 1990s, photographs emerged of the McLaren cars mid-corner with just the rear discs aglow. The team had developed a cunning system that was operated by a second brake pedal in the cockpit; this enabled drivers to add to the braking force on one of the rear wheels, thereby making the car turn more sharply into the corner.

GROUND EFFECT

In the late 1970s, the Lotus team found a way to set up a low-pressure area underneath a car by sealing the gap between it and the track surface and then accelerating the airflow through that channel. At speed, the car was in effect pressed downward, enabling it to go around corners quicker. Others copied and improved on the idea and new technological competition developed. It took the Federation Internationale de l'Automobile (FIA) several years to ban this innovation effectively, since teams kept finding loopholes and workarounds. The adoption of flat bottoms on all cars as mandatory from 1983 onward finally defeated attempts to design with the ground effect.

MOVEABLE AERODYNAMICS

It's possible to design wings so that they flex at high speeds, reducing drag. This is frowned upon, and the FIA polices it with stringent deflection tests.

GLOSSARY

BRAKE BALANCE: The proportion of braking effort is split between the front and back wheels, something that can be adjusted from the cockpit if the driver finds the front or rear wheels are locking up under braking.

CARBON FIBER: A composite material based around strands of carbon woven together to form a fabric, carbon fiber can be cut, layered, glued, and "baked" under pressure to form a light, solid, strong component. Most contemporary F1 cars are made from carbon fiber, including the suspension wishbones, with occasional metal bonded in for added strength.

CFD: Computational fluid dynamics provide a virtual wind tunnel. The design of proto-type components can be tested with software that simulates the flow of fluid over them.

DIFFUSER: An aerodynamic component mounted under a vehicle's floor between the rear wheels, the diffuser is designed to accelerate the air flowing through it.

DOWNFORCE: Also known as negative lift, this is downward pressure on a car and its tires, created by the action of its wings.

DRS: Introduced in 2011, the drag reduction system is a driver-controlled device that opens a flap on the rear wing to boost top speed and create overtaking opportunities. It may only be used in specific areas of a circuit during a race, provided the pursuing car is within a second of the one in front as they pass through a detection zone.

ECU: The engine control unit manages all electronic functions of the car. Since 2008, this has been a standardized component that prevents competitors from using illegal systems, such as traction control.

ERS: The blanket term for various energy recovery systems found on a modern hybrid F1 engine, an ERS helps scavenge energy that would otherwise be dissipated as heat from the brakes and turbocharger.

FLOW CONDITIONER: This aerodynamic device doesn't necessarily create downforce; instead, it directs the air around a vehicle or sets up a vortex to accelerate airflow.

FUEL FLOW: To prevent short bursts of performance (for instance, boosting power to overtake), the flow of fuel is capped at 100 kilograms per hour and monitored through-out a race. Fuel-flow controls are like a dimmer switch in a domestic lighting system: the brighter you allow the bulb to glow, the more energy it uses.

HANDLING BALANCE: While some drivers may prefer a car that tends toward under-steer or oversteer, most prefer their car to behave in a neutral and progressive way as it reaches the limit of grip.

IGNITION MAPPING: Inside the engine, the amount of fuel delivered to the cylinder and the timing of the spark that detonates it can be altered, usually to change the balance of power versus economy. The software governing this balance is called the ignition map.

LADDER: An old-fashioned method of chassis construction used until the late 1950s, based on two parallel rails connected by crossbeams. In plan view, it resembles a ladder.

LAUNCH CONTROL: Currently illegal, this is a system that detects wheelspin when the car is accelerating from a standstill and cuts the power momentarily to counteract it, potentially giving the driver an advantage.

MONOCOQUE: A type of vehicle construction in which the outer skin is integral to the chassis and absorbs some of the loads acting on it.

OVERSTEER: This effect occurs when a car's rear wheels lose adhesion first upon reaching the limit of its cornering grip, which forces the back of the car to slide outwards.

PLANK: This is literally a wooden plank that is attached to the bottom of a car. It is a low-tech but effective way to prevent teams from running their cars too low to the ground, which can be dangerous in wet conditions. The plank is checked for excess wear after a race.

SEMI-AUTOMATIC GEARBOX: A hybrid of automatic and manual gearshift, a semi-automatic gearbox is used to change ratio by means of a paddle-shift mounted behind the steering wheel. Contemporary F1 cars have eight forward gears.

SPACE FRAME: A type of chassis construction used until the 1960s, the space frame was based on aeronautical principles, using a network of thin tubes.

TRACTION CONTROL: Currently illegal, this system identifies wheelspin under acceleration from corners and briefly cuts the engine's power.

TUB: The central section of a modern F1 chassis, the tub is the area in which the driver sits.

TURBOCHARGER: A type of pump driven by the exhaust gas, the turbocharger compresses air going into the engine to create a bigger bang.

UNDERSTEER: Understeering occurs when a vehicle's front wheels lose grip first in a corner and the nose of the car begins to slide wide.

WIND TUNNEL: A wind tunnel is an airflow testing device in which the passage of air over a scale model of a car can be analyzed.

DRIVERS

DRIVERS
TRAINING FOR SUCCESS

FUN FACT

A team boss once told six-foot one-inch Alexander Wurz, now retired, that he should consider having an operation on his legs to shorten them.

HISTORICAL TIDBIT

Sometimes drivers have to go beyond the call of duty. When Jack Brabham ran out of fuel at the end of the 1959 US Grand Prix at Sebring, he jumped out of the car and pushed it across the finish line, claiming fourth place and netting enough points to win the world championship.

KEY PERSON

Michael Schumacher was the real game-changer when it came to driver fitness. Until he came along, many drivers spent their winters lazing on the beach. Schumacher's approach to fitness, and his success, forced his rivals to follow his lead.

You might think driving a car is a low-energy pursuit, but racing a Formula 1 car for up to two hours is a very different matter. F1 drivers must achieve fitness levels similar to athletes to build the strength and stamina to survive the rigors of a race—which means training like athletes do.

F1 cars aren't built for comfort. There's very little compliance in the suspension; the seat is hard carbon-fiber shell; and, once at racing speed, the driver is hit by forces many times that of gravity as the car accelerates, decelerates, and goes around corners. For example, because of the effect of engine braking, aerodynamic downforce, and energy-recovery systems, simply lifting your foot off the throttle while travelling at speed makes the car slow down sharply—about as much as if you hit the brakes in your road car hard enough to make all the wheels lock up. And that's *before* the F1 driver starts braking.

At Monza in Italy, for example, the cars must slow from over 200 miles per hour to just 30 miles per hour for the first turn. That takes just 100 meters and around 1.9 seconds, during which the driver is subjected to over five times the force of gravity while standing on the (unassisted) brake pedal with a pressure equivalent to doing a 135-kilogram single-leg press in the gym.

Cornering forces also put the drivers through levels of physical stress common to fighter pilots, particularly in the neck area. Drivers target this area in the gym, along with other parts of the body that must grapple with the car—but here they have to be careful: muscle bulk alone isn't the answer. Adding muscle also adds weight, and since the driver is counted as part of the car's minimum weight allowance, heavier drivers can be at a disadvantage.

Cardiovascular fitness is also essential, because drivers have to manage the onboard electronic systems of the car while racing. Fatigue would diminish their ability to do that.

FUN FACT

The famously unlucky Chris Amon led 183 laps without actually winning a Grand Prix.

HISTORICAL TIDBIT

Since 1950 only thirteen drivers have won a race from pole position while leading every lap, and setting the fastest lap in the process. Jim Clark did it eight times; currently active drivers Lewis Hamilton and Sebastian Vettel may yet pass him.

KEY PERSON

John Surtees remains the only world champion on two and four wheels, having won the 1964 F1 World Championship after a successful motorcycling career.

It's common for fans to say that a particular driver lucked into a win, or that he only won the world championship because he had the best car. But Formula 1's list of all-time winners is headed by undisputed greats.

Michael Schumacher is the most successful F1 driver of all time. Over a career in two parts—he retired in 2006, after fifteen years at the top, then made a three-season comeback from 2010–2012—he won seven world titles and ninety-one Grands Prix, and set sixty-eight pole positions and seventy-seven fastest laps.

Schumacher started 306 Grands Prix, second only to his former Ferrari teammate Rubens Barrichello, whose record of 322 starts may stand for some time, since no active driver has reached 300 at the time of publication.

The second most successful driver of all time in terms of wins is Lewis Hamilton, who passed former second-place man Alain Prost's tally of fifty-one victories in 2016; Hamilton still has quite a way to go to match or exceed Schumacher, though. Another currently active driver, Sebastian Vettel, is the fourth most successful, having surpassed the legendary Ayrton Senna's total of forty-one in 2015.

Vettel also has the record for most consecutive wins—nine—set during a dominant 2013 season with the Red Bull team. He beat the previous record of seven, jointly held by Schumacher (2004) and Alberto Ascari and Nico Rosberg.

A three-time champion, Senna is regarded as one of the greatest drivers ever to grace an F1 grid. Had a tragic accident at the 1994 San Marino Grand Prix not ended his life at the age of thirty-four, he likely would have set many record benchmarks much higher.

Some drivers set records that are unlikely to be beaten. Four-time champion Juan Manuel Fangio started 51 races having set pole position in twenty-nine of them, and he won twenty-four. He was also the oldest world champion, being aged forty-six when he lifted the trophy for the last time in 1957.

DRIVERS
SUCCESSES AND FAILURES

FUN FACT

After winning the World Championship in 1997, his debut year, with the Williams team, Jacques Villeneuve never won another race.

HISTORICAL TIDBIT

Success can take time to achieve. Mika Häkkinen deservedly won the World Championship twice (in 1998 and 1999), but it took him ninety-six races to notch up his first Grand Prix win—neatly illustrating our point about having to be in the right place at the right time.

KEY PERSON

Andrea de Cesaris is the man no F1 driver wishes to emulate. He started 208 Grand Prix without winning any of them.

Since Formula 1 is a cooperative effort between a human being and a machine, success depends on the excellence of both coming together at the same time. The best driver in the best car is most likely to win races—provided the car doesn't break down—but there are exceptions that prove the rule.

Equally, there were some outstandingly talented drivers who never quite achieved the success they deserved, usually through being in the wrong place—or, rather, the wrong seat—at the wrong time (we'll detail those later). And, though F1 is mostly a meritocratic domain, since most people reach it through achieving success in junior formula, there have been drivers who should probably have shelved their ambitions before getting there.

Michael Schumacher is a notable success story (we've already seen a few of his records). He was drafted in as a short-notice replacement for another racer who'd been sent to jail, so an element of luck opened the door for him. But he made such an immediate impact on his debut, even though he burned out his clutch on the first lap of the race, that a fight broke out between team bosses to secure his signature on a long-term contract.

More recently, Max Verstappen—the son of one of Schumacher's early teammates—became the subject of a bidding war while still racing in a junior formula. The Red Bull soft drink empire signed him to their young driver program and promoted him to F1 within months at the age of seventeen, before he'd even taken his road-car driving test. He won his first Grand Prix in 2016, aged eighteen.

Just as great drivers can arrive from out of nowhere, others of great pedigree and ability can fail to deliver on expectation. Michael Andretti, son of US racing legend Mario Andretti and a successful Indy Car driver in his own right, had a miserable part-season in F1 in 1993, leaving before the end of the year.

WINNERS WHO NEVER WON

FUN FACT

Australian driver Mark Webber finally won his first Grand Prix on his 130th attempt.

HISTORICAL TIDBIT

The talented Ivan Capelli never got the equipment he deserved, but he came within three laps of winning the 1990 French Grand Prix in the unfancied Leyton House car. Capelli led from lap 30 to 77—until his oil pump failed.

KEY PERSON

Stuart Lewis-Evans was another talent never to win a Grand Prix. His tragic death in 1958 led his Vanwall team to quit the sport, leaving Stirling Moss without a "factory" contract for 1959. This also changed the outlook of his manager, Bernie Ecclestone, a man destined for bigger things in F1.

Some believe that Stirling Moss would have been a more deserving winner of the 1958 World Championship than Mike Hawthorn. Indeed, he probably *should* have won it—Hawthorn had briefly driven the wrong way up the track to rejoin after spinning off at the Portuguese Grand Prix, and Moss would have been well within his rights to protest the result and have Hawthorn disqualified.

Being a gentleman, Moss did no such thing. Although he won the last round of the season and netted an extra point by setting fastest lap, he missed the title by one point. Circumstances meant he never got that close again, although he finished third in 1959, 1960, and 1961.

In all, Moss scored sixteen victories in the sixty-six world championship races he started before an injury brought his racing career to a premature halt in 1962. Beyond F1, he won the Mille Miglia road race, many non-championship F1 events, and in sports cars won the Le Mans 24 Hours once and the Sebring 12 Hours twice. Not for nothing is he regarded as the greatest driver never to win the F1 world championship.

Moss is at the head of a decidedly small category. A separate but related one is perhaps sadder still: great drivers who never even managed to win a Grand Prix. On pole position here is New Zealander Chris Amon, of whom Mario Andretti once remarked, "If he became an undertaker, people would give up dying."

Amon won major sports car events, but luck was never on his side in F1. In 1971, he was leading the Italian Grand Prix in a Matra when his visor parted company with his crash helmet; and, in 1972, he was well in front of the field in the French Grand Prix when he picked up a puncture. Amon, though, disputed the "unlucky" tag, pointing out that he had lived in an era when many of his friends had died in accidents.

DRIVERS
RACING INTO RETIREMENT

FUN FACT

Jody Scheckter, the 1979 world champion, has possibly the most unusual post-F1 career: he founded a weapons-training business in his native South Africa, sold it twelve years later, and now owns an organic farm in the UK.

HISTORICAL TIDBIT

During practice for the 1979 Canadian Grand Prix, Niki Lauda—already a double world champion—announced that he was "bored with driving around in circles." He took the next flight home and didn't drive an F1 car again until he was persuaded to come out of retirement in 1982.

KEY PERSON

For Michael Schumacher fans, the boo-hiss bad guy is former Ferrari boss Luca di Montezemolo, who hired Kimi Räikkönen to replace him at the end of 2006.

Racing drivers are super-competitive beasts, and this temperament makes them fundamentally disinclined to go quietly into retirement when the time comes, or even to recognize when that moment has arrived. After a lifetime of racing for a living, occupied by the sport for every waking hour, they simply don't know what to do with themselves.

There are exceptions, of course. Most recently, the 2016 world champion Nico Rosberg announced that he was hanging up his helmet just hours before he collected his trophy. Beating his teammate Lewis Hamilton had required so many sacrifices, explained Rosberg, that he couldn't face doing it again. Alain Prost also quit the sport after winning his fourth title in 1993, though many believe this decision was influenced by the fact that his team had signed his old nemesis, Ayrton Senna, for the following season.

In 2006, after a decade with the Ferrari team in which he won five World Championships for them, Michael Schumacher was nudged ungraciously into retirement by management, who believed that the young Finn Kimi Räikkönen was a better prospect for the future. Schumacher struggled with a post-racing future and took up superbike racing, in which he injured himself several times, before making a three-season F1 comeback for Mercedes. He finally retired in 2012 at the age of forty-three.

Comebacks in general are often inadvisable. Nigel Mansell, the 1992 world champion, went to the US to race in IndyCars in 1993, but was tempted to return part-time for Williams in 1994, after Senna's fatal accident left a vacancy. He planned a full-time comeback in 1995 with McLaren, but the redesigned car that was enlarged to fit him wasn't competitive. He quit after two races.

SHORTEST CAREERS OF ALL TIME

Formula 1 competition is the goal for many racing drivers, but very few of them reach it. Even then, some unfortunate souls fail to make the impact they so greatly desire.

ERNST LOOF

Do-it-yourself racer Loof has the distinction of covering the shortest distance in a race. In 1953, at the age of forty-six, he qualified his self-built Meteor car 31st out of 34 cars on the grid at the German Grand Prix. It was his first and only Grand Prix start, and it didn't take him very far: his fuel pump broke on the grid, so he got no further than a handful of yards.

JEAN-LOUIS SCHLESSER

Schlesser made his Grand Prix debut in Italy in 1988, the day before his fortieth birthday, as a short-notice substitute for Williams driver Nigel Mansell, who was suffering from chicken pox. He had been one of the team's test drivers in 1987 but hadn't been in the cockpit since. Still, he qualified for the race—just—and nearly managed to complete the distance. With one lap to go, he was in 11th place as the race leader, Ayrton Senna, came up to pass him . . . and they collided.

HANS HEYER

A moderately successful touring car driver desperate to participate in an F1 race, one-off German Grand Prix entrant Heyer parked his ATS-Penske at the pit lane exit on race day in 1977, even though he'd failed to qualify. His slim hope was that another entrant's car might break down on the way to the grid and he would be called up as a replacement. This didn't happen, but when two of the frontrunners crashed into one another immediately after the start, Heyer decided to join in anyway, cheered on by his home crowd. His gear selector linkage broke after nine laps, to the great relief of the race stewards.

GLOSSARY

FASTEST LAP

Today, points aren't awarded for setting the fastest lap time in a race (although they were in 1950–1959), but drivers like to set that goal as a badge of honor. In recent years, the sport's official logistics partner—DHL—has sponsored a trophy awarded to the driver who has set the most fastest laps over the course of a season. The optimum time for logging a fast lap is generally toward the end of a race, when the car has less fuel aboard and the ambient temperature and track conditions are most favorable.

G-FORCE

A form of acceleration produced by mechanical force, g-force is expressed as a multiple of standard gravity. When a Formula 1 car brakes, accelerates, or goes around a corner, its mechanical components and the driver experience this movement as a sensation of weight.

INDY CARS

These vehicles are considered the premier category of single-seater racing in the US. Some drivers have "swapped codes" with great success, including Nigel Mansell, Jacques Villeneuve, and Juan Pablo Montoya; others have been less successful.

LEYTON HOUSE

This Japanese real estate company sponsored, then bought, the March Formula 1 team during Japan's property boom in the late 1980s. Notable mostly for allowing design genius Adrian Newey his first opportunity to create an F1 car, Leyton House collapsed when the owner was implicated in a financial scandal and arrested.

MILLE MIGLIA

This famous Italian endurance race is set on a road course of around 1,000 miles, hence the Italian name (which translates as "a thousand miles"). Many F1 and prewar Grand Prix drivers entered it, and their names dominate the winners' list. Since drivers in this era were paid by individual race promoters for appearing, rather than receiving a salary from an employer, it was not unusual to see names from F1 appearing in rallies and sports car events as well as single-seaters.

NON-CHAMPIONSHIP RACES

Before F1 became a globally televised sport commanding billions in sponsorship money, it was rather less structured. Any promoter could lay on an event open to F1 cars; if they could put enough prize money together to make attendance worthwhile, the teams would come. Non-championship races began to fade from the scene during the 1960s, although UK-based events such as the Daily Express Trophy (at Silverstone), the Race of Champions (at Brands Hatch), and the Oulton Park Gold Cup persisted until the 1970s.

SUPERBIKES

A production-based racing category for motorcycles, Superbikes enjoyed Michael Schumacher as a notable convert after his first retirement from F1.

VANWALL

The first winner of the constructors' championship was a British prestige project led by industrialist Tony Vandervell, initially to promote his company's patented Thin Wall bearings.

WILLIAMS

Sir Frank Williams founded his eponymous team in 1977, though he had been entering cars in F1 since 1969. It is one of the most successful outfits in the sport, and the only one remaining in which the person whose name is above the door remains the majority owner.

RIVALRIES

JUAN FANGIO vs. GIUSEPPE FARINA

FUN FACT

Farina only won a single Grand Prix in 1951, after Fangio had to stop in the pits for a quarter of an hour in Belgium.

HISTORICAL TIDBIT

Fangio got off the starting line so quickly in the 1950 Monaco Grand Prix that Farina lost control and spun at the first corner, causing a massive pileup that blocked the circuit—although Fangio somehow managed to thread his way through when he arrived on the scene next time around.

KEY PERSON

Gioacchino Colombo designed the engine of the Alfa Romeo 158s that Farina and Fangio used to claim the world title in 1950 and 1951. The cars had been built in the prewar period and hidden during the hostilities.

A Hollywood movie producer might be tempted to recast the first great rivalry of the Formula 1 World Championship as a tale of a young buck knocking the established figure off his perch, but incumbent star Giuseppe Farina was closing in on his forty-fourth birthday when he clinched the inaugural world title in September 1950, and Juan Manuel Fangio was hardly in the first flush of youth.

Argentine ace Fangio was just five years Farina's junior and hadn't competed on European soil until his thirty-seventh birthday. World War II had cost both men the years when they should have hit peak racing form, though Fangio had kept himself sharp in regional events in South America. Both men hit the scene hard, as motorsport gradually wound back into gear during the late 1940s.

Fangio's sharp-edged competitive streak came wrapped in a comforting shroud of affability and genteel good manners. Farina hailed from more privileged stock, was sure of his place in the world, and bore himself with suitable aristocratic hauteur when in the company of social inferiors.

Their skill sets were also poles apart. What Farina lacked in driving finesse, compared with natural talents such as Fangio, he compensated for with a bravery that verged on the suicidal. Enzo Ferrari once said, "He was like a high-strung thoroughbred, capable of committing the most astonishing follies. As a consequence, he was a regular inmate of the hospital wards."

Farina was Fangio's team leader at Alfa Romeo in 1950 and 1951, and they won three races each. Farina lifted the title by finishing fourth in Belgium, while Fangio failed to score in the rounds Farina won. But Fangio was clearly the faster driver, and he ceased to defer to his team leader when he exerted his authority on the track throughout 1951.

For all the on-track animus, this was a polite rivalry, based on respect: when Fangio was at death's door after a crash in Italy in 1952, Farina visited him in hospital and gave him the winner's laurel wreath.

RIVALRIES
MIKE HAWTHORN vs. STIRLING MOSS

FUN FACT

The 1958 championship finale was the only time Morocco hosted a World Championship F1 race.

HISTORICAL TIDBIT

The Constructors' Championship was inaugurated in 1958 and went to Vanwall. The team quickly faded after this season, and the death of the team's third driver, Stuart Lewis-Evans, sapped owner Tony Vandervell's will to continue in motor racing.

KEY PERSON

Moss's teammate and dutiful number two in 1958 was Tony Brooks, who had the unusual (for a racing driver) distinction of being a qualified dentist. He moved to Ferrari in 1959, taking Hawthorn's place.

In 1958, a small island was gripped by Formula 1 as two of its sons grappled with one another to claim the world title. Fittingly, since the island in question was Great Britain, they acted out the drama in an utterly gentlemanly fashion, thus both thrilling the nation and reinforcing its favored national stereotype.

Stirling Craufurd Moss and John Michael "Mike" Hawthorn epitomized dashing, homegrown heroes: both were from respectable backgrounds and plummily well-spoken, but had earned underdog credentials as they worked their way up from the junior formulae on merit. For a long time, in fact, Hawthorn had raced while wearing a bow tie.

They were very different characters, though. Moss took a hard-bitten professional attitude to his racing, and, though he was happy to have fun and womanize off track, he had no taste for alcohol. Hawthorn was an altogether more rebellious figure who raced hard and played hard.

There was no rancor in their rivalry. In 1958, Hawthorn was driving for Ferrari, Moss for Vanwall, and, although Moss won four races to Hawthorn's one, a better record of points finishes dropped the title in Hawthorn's lap. Second place to Moss in the final round was enough to seal the deal. Famously, Moss turned down the opportunity to lodge a protest against Hawthorn, when his rival drove against the flow of traffic to rejoin the circuit after a spin in Portugal; in fact, he actively lobbied on Hawthorn's behalf.

"The sportsmanship and friendly spirit that Moss and Hawthorn have shown to the other throughout the season has been a pleasure to watch," purred the report in *Autocar*, "and should settle once and for all any suggestion that motor racing is a cut-throat business in which there is little room for finer feelings and good sportsmanship."

The new world champion had already decided to quit, though, after the death of his great friend and teammate Peter Collins some months earlier.

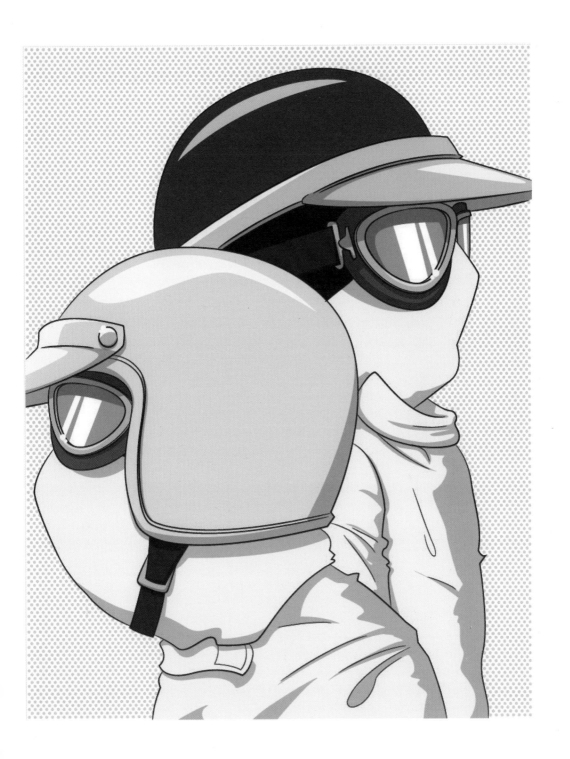

JIM CLARK vs. GRAHAM HILL

FUN FACT

Jim Clark is the only driver to win the F1 World Championship and the Indianapolis 500 in the same year.

HISTORICAL TIDBIT

When the maximum engine displacement in F1 doubled to three liters in 1966, BRM tried to create an "H-16" engine. In effect, it was two of the 1.5-liter V-8s, with the vee angle flattened out somewhat and mated at the crank. The only person to win a race with it was . . . Clark, after Lotus used the engine for a handful of Grands Prix.

KEY PERSON

Tony Rudd was put in charge of engineering at BRM after Hill and Gurney threatened to go on strike. He presided over what proved to be a relatively short-lived turnaround in the team's fortunes in the mid-1960s.

For not many reasons that were good, 1961 saw the capping of F1 engines at 1.5 liters. Ferrari already had a competitive Formula 2 engine that would suit, the other manufacturers—mostly British—less so. Ferrari's dominance that year didn't promise classic racing in the seasons to come.

And yet the following years proved to be remarkable, as the sharpest teams found inventive means of getting around the lack of power and new driving talents came to the fore. In 1962, Lotus produced the 25, F1's first monocoque chassis design, while British Racing Motors (BRM)—for many years a laughingstock—finally came good by pairing the tidy P57 car with a decently powerful V-8 engine.

To this interesting machinery, add two fascinating characters. Former Royal Navy engineer Graham Hill hadn't passed his driving test until the age of twenty-four, at which point he discovered a taste for racing—after talking his way into a job as a racing instructor. It was Hill who instigated the turnaround at BRM after he and his then-teammate Dan Gurney had threatened to go on strike unless a competent engineer was put in charge.

Hill's opponent, Jim Clark, had grown up on a sheep farm on the Scottish border but was a remarkable talent behind the wheel, and his performances in sports cars caught the eye of Lotus founder Colin Chapman.

The 1962 championship went down to the wire. Each driver had won three races as they arrived at the final round, in South Africa, on December 29. Clark started on pole and led throughout, until an oil leak forced him to stop, handing the title to Hill.

In 1963, the momentum went to Clark as BRM's new monocoque-chassis P61 proved not up to scratch. The following year brought a three-way contest in which Hill and Clark were mugged by Ferrari's John Surtees at the final round.

The competition was fierce. After Clark nursed his car home with a sickly engine in the 1965 British Grand Prix, he said, "I would have been prepared to risk 'blowing up' rather than seeing Graham pass me."

JACKIE STEWART vs. JIM CLARK

FUN FACT

Stewart turned down an offer from Lotus for 1965, choosing to drive for BRM instead. He thought being Clark's teammate in his first year in F1 would be a mistake.

HISTORICAL TIDBIT

Clark had a historic aversion to the Spa-Francorchamps circuit after having to swerve to avoid the corpse of a fellow driver there in 1960, yet he won the 1963 race there in wet conditions by nearly five minutes. Stewart had a similar dislike of the Nürburgring.

KEY PERSON

Walter Hayes was the Ford PR guru who signed off the Cosworth-developed Ford DFV engine that took Clark to his final World Championship in 1967. It also powered Stewart to all three of his drivers' titles.

It's a sign of how highly regarded Clark was that even his rivals—those still with us to tell the tale, that is—regard themselves as having been in his shadow. In 1965, Jackie Stewart was the hot new talent on the scene. He was Hill's teammate at BRM, but he performed very much on terms with him on pace. For three Grands Prix that summer, Stewart finished second to Clark, until he finally put one over on him at Monza—and then only after Clark had dropped out with a broken fuel pump.

"We were like Batman and Robin," said Stewart of his friend and fellow Scot. "And there was no doubt who was Batman and who was Robin."

Considering Stewart's sublime talent—he would go on to become world champion three times—this is quite a statement.

Clark and Stewart differed in personality. Clark was charismatic but never lost an edge of shyness, which drove him to shield himself from his increasing fame. At heart he was still a boy from a sheep farm. Stewart had grown up with dyslexia at a time when the condition wasn't fully understood; as a consequence, he had been treated poorly by the British education system. As is the way with such things, his personality had worked around the problem like a river finding its natural course. He had star quality and embraced fame.

Circumstances prevented their rivalry from blossoming into something truly epic on track. When Lotus were at their peak, Clark was utterly dominant.

Still, this was a rivalry to savor. Stewart loves to tell the story about the time his throttle stuck open at Monza during practice, and it took every ounce of his skill to make it round the Curva Grande corner. After listening to Stewart regale his fellow drivers about the moment, Clark piped up: "Are you saying, Jackie, that you normally lift off there?"

EMERSON FITTIPALDI vs. CLAY REGAZZONI

FUN FACT

Fittipaldi had a career of two halves. After an epiphany at the end of the 1975 season he left McLaren to form a new all-Brazilian team with his older brother, Wilson. Over the next five years he managed just one podium finish.

HISTORICAL TIDBIT

New Zealander Bruce McLaren founded McLaren after he realized he could build a better car than the ones he was being given by his Cooper team. McLaren was killed testing a Can-Am car in 1970.

KEY PERSON

Luca di Montezemolo was brought in by Enzo Ferrari to turn his struggling team around for the 1974 season. It was he who hired Regazzoni—who had driven for Ferrari before—as well as Niki Lauda, who would go on to be champion in 1975 and 1977.

From the moment he touched down on European soil, Brazilian Emerson Fittipaldi was on the fast-track to greatness. In 1969 he was queuing up for Graham Hill's autograph; a year later he was the third driver for Lotus in F1, then rapidly promoted to team leader after the death of Jochen Rindt; and in 1972 he became the sport's youngest ever world champion at the age of twenty-five, a record that would stand until 2006.

From that point on, Fittipaldi's outlook changed. He continued to have a good turn of speed, but he preferred to play the percentages and win through guile rather than pushing the performance envelope of his cars. Clay Regazzoni had no such qualms. Enzo Ferrari described the dashing Swiss as a "dancer, viveur, playboy, and a driver in his spare time." He was perhaps not as quick as Fittipaldi, but his aggression behind the wheel put him in the same drawer as Giuseppe Farina. After an on-track encounter at Monza in 1970, Jackie Stewart described his driving as "unethical, unsporting, and dangerous."

In 1974 they both had similarly competitive machinery at the same time, Fittipaldi in a McLaren M23 and Regazzoni in a Ferrari 312B3. It had been a competitive season with seven different winners, but Fittipaldi came to the final round at Watkins Glen ahead in the title battle—by just a single point from "Regga."

They qualified eighth and ninth but Regazzoni got ahead at the start, then swerved while trying to pass Fittipaldi, forcing the Brazilian off the track. This time, rather than back off and play the percentages, Fittipaldi held his nerve, bounced back onto the track, banged wheels with his rival, and forced his way past.

"He was never expecting to get this reaction from me," said the new world champion.

FUN FACT

The Hunt-Lauda rivalry draws so much attention that people often forget who actually won the dramatic final race of the 1976 season: Mario Andretti, in a Lotus.

HISTORICAL TIDBIT

In 1976 the FIA decided to clamp down on the trend for increasingly large (and ugly) engine air intakes on the cars, but set a rather badly thought-out date to start the ban: May 1. That resulted not just in three races being run *with* the big airboxes, but since the Spanish GP was on Sunday, May 2, teams practiced with them on the Friday before taking them off.

KEY PERSON

Dave Morgan was the driver Hunt punched after the two collided in a Formula 3 race in Crystal Palace in 1970. The movie *Rush* fictionalized the event, making the altercation between Hunt and Lauda.

The tale of the showdown for the 1976 world championship sounds like the plot of a Hollywood movie. Eventually it eventually became one: *Rush*, 2013.

Niki Lauda's wealthy family disowned his racing activities, and the Austrian had to take out a bank loan to fund his early career. Even then, he was viewed as a no-mark pay driver until he gained a reputation for being focused, no-nonsense, very fast, and excellent at developing cars to make them better. After joining Ferrari during one of the team's periodic dips in form, he played a key role in turning things around.

James Hunt was a far more mercurial character, and from a far less financially privileged background than his immaculate public-school accent would suggest. Nerves often got the better of him before races, and in the junior formulae he earned the nickname "Hunt the Shunt" after a series of crashes. He initially made it to F1 with the Hesketh team, run by a bunch of aristocratic good-time boys.

In 1976 Lauda was the sitting world champion and Hunt had only remained in the sport by good fortune—Hesketh had closed down, but McLaren needed a driver at short notice after Emerson Fittipaldi quit. Lauda and Hunt enjoyed relatively cordial relations, but their teams were almost implacable enemies. Ferrari schemed to have Hunt disqualified on a small technicality from a race he'd won, and he was only reinstated months later after an appeal.

Lauda had a horrific accident at the Nürbrurging, suffering life-threatening burns that scarred him for life. Yet by sheer force of will he returned to the cockpit at the Italian Grand Prix and reached the final race of the season, in Japan, three points ahead of Hunt.

Torrential rain on race day should have been sufficient grounds to delay or cancel, but the TV cameras were rolling and the race went ahead. On the second lap Lauda decided it was too dangerous and quit the race. Hunt finished in third place, which was enough to win the title.

ALAN JONES vs. CARLOS REUTEMANN

FUN FACT

Reutemann would have been the 1981 world champion if points from the South African Grand Prix, which he won, had been awarded. A political war between the teams and the governing body led to it losing its world championship status.

HISTORICAL TIDBIT

The Caesar's Palace Grand Prix in Las Vegas, scene of the 1981 title showdown, was one of those ideas that must have seemed great at the time. Drivers disliked the circuit, a temporary setup in the casino's vast car park, and such were the city's many distractions that the race drew only a small crowd.

KEY PERSON

Mechanic Giovanni Amadeo was fatally injured when he fell off the pitwall into the path of Reutemann's Williams during practice for the 1981 Belgian Grand Prix. The incident is believed to contributed to Reutemann's decision to retire from the sport.

Sometimes teammates clash because their personalities are similar. Other times they quarrel because their characters are so entirely removed that they were always destined to mix like oil and water. And so it was with tough, hard-charging, frank-speaking Australian Alan Jones and the gifted but enigmatic Argentine Carlos Reutemann.

Reutemann's career is an enduring mystery. Fast and deft behind the wheel, he frustrated team owners who could never be sure which Reutemann would be arriving for work on any given day: the unbeatable one, or the distracted and unmotivated one whose head simply wasn't in the zone. When he arrived at Williams in 1980 he was eight years into a career in which he'd had competitive cars at Brabham and Ferrari but failed to comprehensively outshine his teammates.

"Carlos needed more psychological support than most drivers," said team owner Frank Williams years later. "We probably didn't appreciate that sufficiently at the time."

Williams wasn't a team in which drivers were mollycoddled. The no-nonsense Jones was precisely the kind of driver Williams and his business partner, the well-respected engineer Patrick Head, preferred to employ. And Jones was explicitly the team's number one driver, winning the world title in 1980.

The relationship between the two men, never warm, hit the irreconcilable differences stage at the beginning of 1981. Feeling that his role in supporting Jones had gone unacknowledged, Reutemann sullenly clung to the lead of the Brazilian Grand Prix in spite of explicit orders to hand it over to his teammate. By the end of the fractious and uncomfortable year it was Reutemann in contention for the title rather than Jones, but after setting pole for the season finale in Las Vegas he went backwards in the race and it slipped from his grasp.

When Reutemann approached Jones to suggest they bury the hatchet, Jones replied, "Yeah—in the back of your bloody head, mate."

GILLES VILLENEUVE vs. DIDIER PIRONI

FUN FACT

Gilles Pironi now works as a design engineer in F1.

HISTORICAL TIDBIT

Only fourteen cars started the fateful 1982 San Marino Grand Prix, owing to a boycott by the teams associated with the Formula One Constructors Association as part of its ongoing war with the governing body.

KEY PERSON

Former Hesketh designer Harvey Postlethwaite was the British designer recruited by Ferrari to improve its technical offering for the 1982 season. Reputedly, he used to keep a slip of paper in his desk drawer with his salary written on it; when the team's internal politics grew intolerable, he would open the drawer to remind himself why he stayed there.

Perhaps no other rivalry in the history of Formula 1 has had such devastating consequences as the bust-up between Ferrari teammates Gilles Villeneuve and Didier Pironi in 1982.

They were friends—close enough for Pironi to name his twin sons Didier and Gilles—but both men had a burning desire to win.

"Gilles was maybe the biggest talent around and he would just invent a way of driving a corner—very spontaneous, very creative," recalled Ferrari's then sporting director, Marco Piccinini. "Didier, though, would assess the risk in a very cool manner, build himself up and start the lap with the sure intention of staying flat through a corner."

Villeneuve's bravura made him the darling of both Enzo Ferrari and the team's legion of fans. Pironi had arrived in the sport via a French racing scholarship program, and had gradually been getting over a reputation for being brave and fast but crash-prone at other teams when he arrived at Ferrari in 1981. The car that year, Ferrari's first with a turbocharged engine, wasn't good, but while Villeneuve outshone Pironi on track, the newcomer was building political alliances within the team.

At first, the apolitical Villeneuve chose to ignore this. For 1982, though, the car was better, and Villeneuve was leading Pironi in the San Marino Grand Prix when the team hung out the "slow" sign with eight laps to go, a prearranged procedure that signaled both drivers to back off and preserve their cars to the finish. Villeneuve obeyed, and Pironi made a spur-of-the-moment decision to overtake him and win the race.

The incident threw Villeneuve into personal turmoil. His immediate feelings of betrayal soured into outright paranoia. And it was in this state of mind, still raging, that he suffered a fatal accident during qualifying for the next Grand Prix.

The anguished Pironi never found peace. While leading the championship standings later in the season he smashed both legs in an accident, ending his driving career.

ALAIN PROST vs. NIKI LAUDA

FUN FACT

The TAG turbo engine was designed and built by Porsche.

HISTORICAL TIDBIT

Half points were awarded for the 1984 Monaco Grand Prix after it was stopped early because of heavy rain. Famously, in the unfancied Toleman car, rookie Ayrton Senna was catching Prost for the race lead; what's less well known was that he had damaged his suspension and probably wouldn't have finished if the race had gone the full distance.

KEY PERSON

John Barnard was the technical architect of the ground-breaking McLaren carbon fiber chassis. After leaving the sport, he moved into high-end furniture design.

In the early 1980s McLaren was a team on the move again after falling into a deep competitive trough in the late 1970s. Title sponsor Marlboro had become twitchy at the lack of success and engineered a merger between McLaren and the up-and-coming Formula 2 team Project Four, led by former Brabham mechanic Ron Dennis.

After a decade of struggling to find the cash to break into F1, Dennis was a man on a mission. The old team management did not stick around for long. Within a few months McLaren had unveiled the first F1 car to be made principally from carbon fiber, while behind the scenes Dennis was sourcing fresh investment from Techniques d'Avant Garde (at that point the TAG in TAG Heuer watches) to buy out his partners and underwrite the development of a new turbocharged 1.5-liter V-6 engine. There was also the question of getting the best drivers.

Dennis charmed double world champion Niki Lauda out of retirement for 1982, and Lauda proved to be competitive, defying expectations and winning one Grand Prix. But the package wasn't complete until '84, when the TAG turbo arrived along with a bespoke new chassis—and Alain Prost.

The French ace had been a talented rookie when he quit McLaren in a funk in 1980. Now he was at the height of his powers and had a point to prove after being fired by his previous team, Renault, for criticizing his car.

Prost played his car like a piano, delicately and with great economy of motion. He rarely looked like he was trying, and yet he would light up the timing screens. More than once, in qualifying, Lauda would exclaim, "Shit! How does he do that?"

Lauda was on the back foot, winning five races (of which four came through Prost having car trouble while ahead). Prost won seven, but by scoring more consistently Lauda beat him to the title by half a point.

Prost was dominant again in 1985 and had better reliability. By season's end Lauda knew he was well beaten, and that it was time to retire for the second and last time.

NIGEL MANSELL vs. NELSON PIQUET

FUN FACT

In 2013 Piquet and Mansell were reunited in an ad campaign for the Ford Fusion car in Brazil. It was clear they still agreed to differ.

HISTORICAL TIDBIT

Williams lost their Honda deal to McLaren for 1988 and had to use naturally aspirated Judd engines. Having been runaway winners of the constructors' title in '87, they slumped to seventh.

KEY PERSON

Piquet and Mansell's team principal was Frank Williams. A keen amateur racer in his early years, he was perfectly happy to let his drivers race rather than institute team orders.

What Formula 1 needed to really join the spirit of the 1980s was to have two rivals publicly spitting at one another in the style of the shoulder-pad-wearing "superbitches" from the TV soaps popular at the time. Nigel Mansell and Nelson Piquet might not have ended up fighting in a lily pond in their party frocks like *Dynasty*'s Alexis Colby and Krystle Carrington, but their mutual loathing was on par for entertainment value and sheer destructiveness.

What made this among the greatest rivalries in F1 history was not just that the action took place both on- and off-track, and in the full glare of the world's media, but also that each driver cost the other a world title. Piquet, arguably, should have clinched it in 1986, and Mansell in 1987. Fortunately for their Williams team, Piquet took the honors in '87; the previous year, Alain Prost had snatched the trophy in the final round.

During those two seasons Williams overtook McLaren as the most competitive outfit, largely on account of the prodigious power output of the new Honda V-6 engine. Piquet was a double world champion when Williams hired him in 1986 and he believed himself to be the team's number one driver. But he'd reckoned without the grit of Mansell, a bull of a man who had mortgaged his house to fund his early career and survived a broken neck.

Mansell's speed gave Piquet a fright and he hit back by targeting Mansell's weak spot: his thin skin. No mind game tactic was off the table so far as Piquet was concerned; he even insulted Mansell's wife in an interview.

They took lumps out of each other on-track, too, such that 1986 ended with neither of them winning the title. In 1987 Mansell had Piquet (who was suffering blurred vision after a crash in San Marino) beaten for speed, then injured himself in Japan and missed the last two rounds, enabling his slower teammate to collect the prize.

RIVALRIES
ALAIN PROST vs. AYRTON SENNA

FUN FACT

In 1988, the first year of the Senna-Prost partnership, McLaren scored three times as many constructors' points as second-place Ferrari.

HISTORICAL TIDBIT

In the early days of F1, if a team's number one driver retired from a race, he was entitled to take over a teammate's car. It didn't always happen: in 1956, Luigi Musso refused to hand his Ferrari over to Juan Manuel Fangio, a move that nearly cost his team leader the World Championship.

KEY PERSON

Ron Dennis entered Formula 1 as a mechanic and went on to become the most successful team leader of all time, winning 158 Grands Prix and seventeen championships with McLaren. He was famous for his obsessive attention to detail and his long-winded way of speaking, known to F1 fans as "Ronspeak."

Having the two best drivers in Formula 1 on the same team, with the best car, must have seemed like a great idea at the time. Unfortunately for McLaren boss Ron Dennis, pairing Brazilian Ayrton Senna with Frenchman Alain Prost for the 1988 season ignited one of the most toxic rivalries of all time.

McLaren had by far the best car, and the drivers were promised equal equipment and equal status. Between them, Senna and Prost won all but one of the sixteen races in that season, and Senna won the drivers' championship with one round still to go.

The brooding, ultra-competitive Senna had a burning desire to test himself against the very best—and defeat them. Prost, who felt that having won two world titles with McLaren entitled him to number one status, was unsettled by Senna's intensity.

In 1989 McLaren again had the best car and the best engine, but the two drivers declared war on each other after an argument over racing etiquette at the San Marino Grand Prix. Each suspected that the other was getting better equipment, so they fell to such pettiness as insisting that engine selection was decided by the flip of a coin.

The title was decided in Prost's favor when the two collided on track during the season finale in Japan. Prost was out on the spot, while Senna got going again and won the race, but was then disqualified.

Prost left to join Ferrari, but that wasn't the end of the war. The Japanese Grand Prix was the theater of conflict again in 1990 as Senna deliberately drove into Prost as they braked from 170 miles per hour for the first corner, a move that could have killed them both.

When Prost was fired by Ferrari for criticizing his car in 1991, and then took the following year as sabbatical, the two were no longer fighting for the same space on the road. Senna found himself missing his rival, and when Prost retired for good after making a championship-winning comeback in 1993, Senna pleaded with him to change his mind.

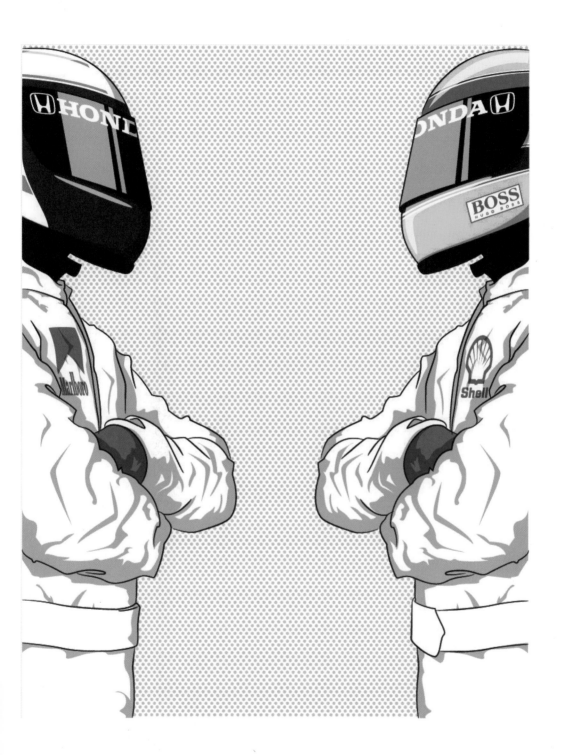

NIGEL MANSELL vs. ALAIN PROST

After winning the drivers' championship with Williams in 1992, Mansell moved to the US to race in IndyCars, winning that championship first time out.

HISTORICAL TIDBIT

At the Mexican Grand Prix in 1990, Mansell completed an extraordinarily brave overtaking move on McLaren's Gerhard Berger at the imposing Peraltada corner. It was such an iconic moment that the corner was subsequently renamed for Mansell when the track was redeveloped.

KEY PERSON

Cesare Fiorio was Ferrari's sporting director and the man caught in the war between his two drivers. Each was sure that he was either not supporting them enough, or was actively conspiring with the other to furnish preferential treatment.

The indomitable Nigel Mansell landed at Ferrari for 1989, tempted by a bold new car designed by ex-McLaren technical director John Barnard, launching himself into the chaos left by marque founder Enzo Ferrari's death the previous autumn. Against the odds—the car was unreliable at first—Mansell seized two improbable victories that year.

Added to that, his combative style sent the team's fans into a state of rapture. They named him *Il Leone*—"the lion."

Imagine Mansell's disquiet, then, when Alain Prost arrived from McLaren for 1990 as sitting world champion, also importing one of McLaren's senior engineers, Steve Nichols. Their driving styles were at opposite ends of the scale: Mansell liked to show a car who was boss, driving around any problems, while Prost preferred to perfect his mechanical setup to make his car sing. Mansell dismissed him as "a chauffeur."

But Prost was also politically sophisticated, and, having moved to Ferrari to get away from Senna, he was ill-disposed toward butting heads with his teammate. No cross words were spoken, but an idea formed in Mansell's head—slowly at first, but then growing and hardening into certainty as each race weekend brought supporting "evidence"—that Prost was pushing team management to throw their weight behind him as the most likely Ferrari driver to win the championship.

Three retirements and just two podium finishes in the first seven races convinced Mansell that he was being given inferior equipment. He has claimed as much in interviews and in his autobiography. At the British Grand Prix, he says, he discovered that his chassis—in which he'd qualified on pole for the preceding race—had been swapped for Prost's without his knowledge, at Prost's request.

So when Mansell's engine failed—again—he got out of the car, somewhat theatrically threw his gloves into the crowd, and announced his retirement from motor racing. It didn't last long. A few months later, he announced his return to Williams for 1991.

DAMON HILL vs. MICHAEL SCHUMACHER

FUN FACT

Formula 1 had two Australian Grands Prix in a row when Adelaide (which hosted the final round of 1995) handed the race over to a new venue in Melbourne (scene of the first race of 1996).

HISTORICAL TIDBIT

Hill's victory at Suzuka in 1996, which decided the drivers' title in his favor, was an emotional moment for many viewers—including venerable British TV commentator Murray Walker. "Damon Hill exits the chicane and wins the Japanese Grand Prix," he told his viewers, "and I've got to stop, because I've got a lump in my throat."

KEY PERSON

David Coulthard had taken over from Hill as Williams' test driver and was promoted to the race team as Hill's number two after Senna's death. He went on to have a successful Grand Prix career in his own right.

Ayrton Senna's fatal accident at San Marino in 1994 thrust his teammate, Damon Hill, into the spotlight as the man who now would lead the title fight against Michael Schumacher. In a year sorely overshadowed by Senna's death—and by suspicions that Schumacher's Benetton team were cheating with illegal electronic systems—Formula 1 needed a stirring narrative. "Senna versus Schumacher" had been prematurely snuffed out. Now, the beleaguered sport's box office was resting on "Hill versus Schumacher."

Hill's father Graham had been twice a world champion. After he crashed his Piper Aztec plane in 1975, killing all aboard, it brought more than just emotional turmoil: subsequent legal action by relatives of the victims cost the Hill family their home. Damon, more thoughtful and less extroverted than his father, had worked as a motorcycle courier before entering the world of motor racing, relatively late in life. He was thirty when Williams employed him as a Formula 1 test driver in 1991.

Schumacher was a young hotshot. He was promoted quickly through the junior formulae with Mercedes patronage, breaking into F1 at the age of twenty-one while Hill was still working behind the scenes at Williams.

When Hill took on the mantle of team leader in May 1994, it set off an extraordinary battle that raged over the remainder of that season and the following two. Hill's grit and quiet dignity in the aftermath of Senna's death, combined with revelations that Benetton's software did indeed contain suspect code—and that they had illegally modified their refueling rigs—set the plucky-Brit-versus-dastardly-German narrative in concrete, at least as far as fans were concerned.

There was mass outrage when Schumacher appeared to deliberately put Hill in the wall at the season-closing Australian Grand Prix, winning the title by a point. But then, poor reliability held Hill back in 1995, and the media began to write him off as a hopeless case. When he beat both Schumacher and his own new teammate, Jacques Villeneuve, to the title in 1996, Hill laid many ghosts to rest.

MIKA HÄKKINEN vs. MICHAEL SCHUMACHER

FUN FACT

The spin at Monza in 1999 that elicited tears was caused by Häkkinen shifting down one gear too many and locking his back wheels.

HISTORICAL TIDBIT

Schumacher won the last Argentine Grand Prix in 1998. The event had returned to the calendar in 1995 after a thirteen-year layoff, but then the organizers failed to agree to terms with the commercial rights holder in 1999. The race was cancelled on short notice, never to occur again.

KEY PERSON

Eddie Irvine was Schumacher's Ferrari teammate until 1999, the year he became Ferrari's de facto drivers' championship hope when Schumacher suffered a broken leg. He fell short, but secured enough points for Ferrari to win the constructors' title for the first time since 1983.

Over the course of four seasons around the turn of the century, the career trajectories of Mika Häkkinen and Michael Schumacher became intertwined to great dramatic effect. Schumacher, twice world champion at Benetton in 1994 and 1995, moved to a Ferrari team that was in one of its competitive slumps. Along with other new personnel—including ex-Benetton engineers Ross Brawn and Rory Byrne—Schumacher was part of a money-is-no-object push to bring Ferrari back to the top.

They began to reach that point just as Häkkinen finally got the car his talent deserved. Like Ferrari, McLaren had been in the doldrums throughout the 1990s, until they recruited the inventive designer Adrian Newey from the Williams team. After six seasons in middling machinery, Häkkinen had a launch pad. Newey came up with the best solution to new technical rules for the 1998 season, and McLaren were dominant over the opening races.

Ferrari came back strongly, though, and Schumacher pushed Häkkinen all the way to the final round. But then he made an uncharacteristic mistake and stalled on the grid. Häkkinen won the race and the championship.

In the following season, McLaren and Ferrari started off more evenly matched, and the outcome might have been different had Schumacher not crashed and broken his leg at Silverstone. While Häkkinen had been racking up pole positions, he wasn't always converting them into victories; car failures and his own small but costly errors at critical moments kept him from winning. He was under pressure, something that was underlined when he spun off at Monza, walked behind a tree, and wept uncontrollably. Still, he put the world title to bed as Schumacher's teammate Eddie Irvine proved inadequate to the challenge.

Poor engine reliability in 2000 cost Häkkinen dearly, but he completed the overtake of the season at Belgium, a heart-stopping move at 200 miles per hour that put Schumacher in his place. It wasn't enough to win the title and, throughout 2001, Häkkinen showed signs of mental exhaustion. At the end of the season, he announced a sabbatical from which he never returned.

MICHAEL SCHUMACHER vs. FERNANDO ALONSO

FUN FACT

At the time of writing, McLaren test driver Pedro de la Rosa holds the lap record for the Bahrain circuit, which he set in 2005—his only start for the team that year. Regular driver Juan Pablo Montoya was sidelined with an injury.

HISTORICAL TIDBIT

Michael Schumacher's one win in 2005 came at the infamous US Grand Prix at Indianapolis, where a stand-off between Michelin and the governing body over safety resulted in all but six of the cars pulling out before the start of the race.

KEY PERSON

Mike Gascoyne was the technical director of Renault in this era, setting up a relatively unusual split design team in which one group began working on the following season's car while the other continued developing the current one.

Having unseated Mika Häkkinen from the World Championship in 2000—and destroying him psychologically along the way—Michael Schumacher went on a victory roll that lasted half a decade. His success delighted fans in his native Germany as well as those who appreciated consistent excellence, but floating voters began to grow a little weary as the tide rose.

There was no stopping Schumacher from 2001 to 2004, either. With the exception of 2003, when the governing body resorted to changing the points system in an effort to close things up, he slam-dunked the drivers' title with several rounds to go. TV viewing figures began to slide and consensus grew that things had to change.

For 2005, the governing body introduced several new rules, most significantly a ban on mid-race tire changes. Ferrari's supplier, Bridgestone, adapted much less well than Michelin, and Schumacher spent the year in the virtual wilderness.

Of the many Michelin-supplied drivers vying for supremacy, Renault's Fernando Alonso came to the fore. The team had been consistently on the up since 2003, when Alonso broke Bruce McLaren's longstanding (since 1959) record for being the youngest Grand Prix winner. Intense, brooding, and hypercompetitive, Alonso won the title with two rounds to go.

In 2006, the no-tire-changes rule was dropped on safety grounds and the season developed into a brutal tussle between Alonso and Schumacher, Renault and Ferrari—on and off the track. At Monaco, Schumacher was castigated for "accidentally" spinning and blocking the track during qualifying, forcing Alonso to abort his lap. Renault were forced to remove a trick suspension system that gave them an advantage, leading to churlish mutterings that Ferrari were being given favorable treatment by the governing body.

The two drivers won seven races each. Although it seemed as if everything was stacked against him, Alonso had scored more consistently and claimed the title. The Michael Schumacher era was definitively over.

FERNANDO ALONSO vs. LEWIS HAMILTON

FUN FACT

For the first season in over twenty years, 2007 saw three drivers entering the final race with a shot at the title. Mathematically, the man least likely to do it—Ferrari's Kimi Räikkönen—actually won, ahead of Alonso and Hamilton.

HISTORICAL TIDBIT

"Spygate" exploded when McLaren designer Mike Coughlan sent his wife to photocopy the tranche of Ferrari documentation he'd obtained. An employee of the copy shop tipped off Ferrari.

KEY PERSON

FIA president Max Mosley, a bitter enemy of McLaren boss Ron Dennis, took center stage in the 2007 season as he pursued the "Spygate" case, finally handing the team a record $100 million fine and cancelling its constructors' championship points.

Combining the hottest established talent with a promising rookie that McLaren had been grooming for over a decade ought to have created a winning combination. Instead, the partnership of Fernando Alonso and Lewis Hamilton in 2007 resulted in unprecedented rancor, magnifying the impact of a damaging scandal that left the team $100 million poorer. It could not have gone more wrong.

Alonso had been managed by Renault team principal Flavio Briatore, but he wanted to control his own destiny. As such, at the end of the 2005 season—having just won the world title for the first time with Renault—he privately concluded a deal with McLaren's Ron Dennis to jump ship for 2007. At the same time, Hamilton was on the fast-track to F1 stardom. He had been under McLaren's wing ever since he cheekily introduced himself to Dennis at an awards ceremony, at the age of ten, in 1995.

Within weeks of the 2007 season start, the cozy arrangement was falling apart. Dennis had led Alonso to believe that he would be the number one driver; instead, the world champion found himself partnered with an ambitious rookie who was thoroughly embedded in the McLaren world and expecting—and receiving—equal treatment. Hamilton was also fast enough to give Alonso a fright, finishing closely behind him in the first two races and then ahead in the following two.

A situation similar to that between Ayrton Senna and Alain Prost developed, one so dysfunctional that the two drivers actively sought to sabotage one another. In public, it came to a head during qualifying for the Hungarian Grand Prix when Alonso spoiled Hamilton's final run.

Alonso also threatened to approach the FIA with damaging information relating to the growing "Spygate" scandal, in which a McLaren designer had illicitly obtained Ferrari designs. This forced Dennis to contact the FIA and begin to backtrack on earlier denials, opening the door to further action.

Fittingly, perhaps, with each having damaged the other's prospects, neither Alonso nor Hamilton won the world title that season.

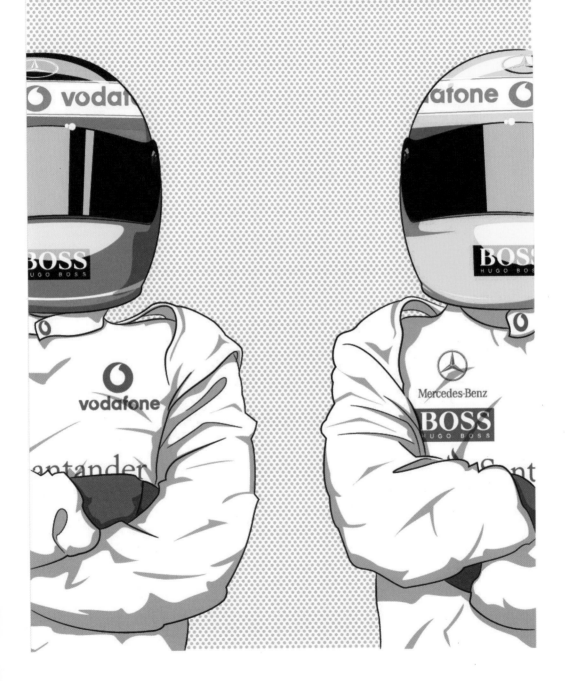

MARK WEBBER vs. SEBASTIAN VETTEL

FUN FACT

Vettel claims to be a fan of classic British comedy shows, such as *Monty Python's Flying Circus*.

HISTORICAL TIDBIT

Webber alleges in his autobiography that Vettel sent a two-page lawyer's letter to the Red Bull team after Malaysia 2013, accusing them of breaching his contract by trying to impose team orders.

KEY PERSON

Former Grand Prix driver Helmut Marko is Red Bull's "driver adviser." He has the ear of Red Bull magnate Dietrich Mateschitz and supervises hirings and firings on the young driver program.

Australian Mark Webber had overcome many obstacles during his career, from lack of finance early on to the persistent trouble of fitting his tall frame into the tight space of a single-seater race car. But when he finally got himself into race-winning machinery, he faced the toughest challenge of all: being partnered with his team's favorite son.

Red Bull had been involved in Formula 1 for several years as a sponsor when they finally took the plunge and bought a team outright in 2005. Webber came on board in 2007, and results gradually began to improve as the team's technical offering matured, thanks to another key signing, design genius Adrian Newey.

The angst began in 2009, when Webber was joined by Sebastian Vettel, one of the latest prodigies from Red Bull's young driver program. Unlike many of his predecessors, the twenty-one-year-old German was no slouch, and already a Grand Prix winner. Webber, now well into his thirties, was used to psychologically intimidating his younger teammates; none of his tricks worked on Vettel, though.

Red Bull were competitive in 2009, and Vettel finished second in the drivers' standings. But for the following season—and the three after that—they had by far the best car. That was when relations between the drivers really went south, as the idea lodged in Webber's head that he was seen as second best.

The conflict soon went public. In 2010, they took each other out of the race in Turkey while running first and second, then raged at each other afterwards. At Silverstone, Red Bull had newly redesigned front wings for both cars. Vettel damaged his, so the team replaced it with the one from Webber's car. After winning the race, Webber vented his anger on the radio: "Not bad for a number two driver . . . ."

Imposing team orders didn't help: Vettel ignored them, passing Webber during the 2013 Malaysian Grand Prix. He escaped with a slapped wrist. Webber retired at the end of the season.

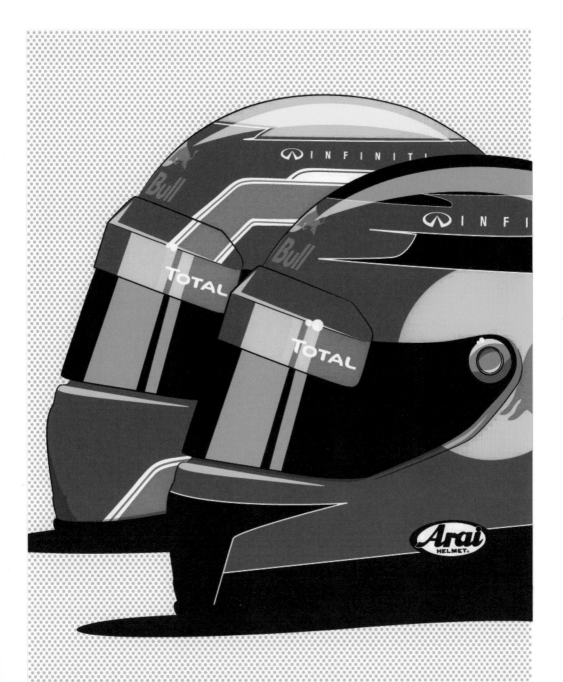

LEWIS HAMILTON vs. NICO ROSBERG

FUN FACT

Teams that get a jump on others after rule changes usually become less dominant in the following seasons, as their rivals catch up. Mercedes actually got *more* successful, winning all but two rounds in 2016.

HISTORICAL TIDBIT

The decision to bring TV cameras into the "green room" before post-race podium ceremonies enabled viewers to get inside a rivalry as never before. Often, the tension was palpable as Hamilton and Rosberg did their best to ignore one another. Was it like this in years past, when this part of the race day went unscreened?

KEY PERSON

Mercedes team boss Toto Wolff had the unenviable task of trying to stop his drivers taking lumps out of one another. By and large, he succeeded.

Nico Rosberg, son of the 1982 world champion, was born into a privileged Monaco lifestyle, and was bright and well educated. Meanwhile, Lewis Hamilton's father worked two jobs to fund his son's karting career. They were teammates during those karting years, and, if Lewis was usually the more successful of the two, that didn't seem to get in the way of their friendship.

Being teammates in the best outfit in Formula 1 did.

Mercedes had built relentlessly toward the 2014 season and for the next three seasons the team enjoyed a supremacy that almost defied belief.

The relationship between Hamilton and Rosberg could not survive it.

The first tremors had been felt in 2013, when Rosberg grudgingly respected a team order not to pass Hamilton during the Malaysian Grand Prix when he felt he was much faster.

At Monaco in 2014, Rosberg made a "mistake" in qualifying and went down an escape road, spoiling Hamilton's lap. Rosberg duly started on pole and won. The two pointedly didn't shake hands or acknowledge one another afterward. This was the first public show of ill will, but it later emerged that each driver had used unauthorized engine modes for a power boost to hold off the other in previous races.

The team struggled to contain the situation. In Belgium, Rosberg and Hamilton collided on the second lap, and now team boss Toto Wolff said there would be "consequences."

Hamilton won the title in 2014 and 2015, but some poor reliability—which he hinted on social media was caused by Mercedes favoring his teammate—swung the balance Rosberg's way in 2016. The stress and effort of these years had worn heavily on the new champion, and he decided to quit while he was ahead, announcing his retirement just before collecting his trophy.

WHY TEAMMATES ARE OFTEN THE BEST OF ENEMIES

"Mon ami, mate" was the warm and cheery phrase with which friends—and, later, Ferrari teammates—Peter Collins and Mike Hawthorn would greet one another in the 1950s. Their off-track exploits became the stuff of legend, and the death of Collins in a crash in 1958 is thought to have been one of the prime motivations for Hawthorn's decision to retire at the end of that season. In an era in which drivers were under less time pressure from media and sponsors, and in which they generally socialized with each other much more than today, the camaraderie between Hawthorn and Collins wasn't unusual.

Tempting though it is to suggest that intrateam rancor is a modern invention, dig deeper into the past and you find ample evidence that not all teammates got along. It's been claimed, for instance, that while Hawthorn and Collins were best buddies and continued to be so while driving together at Ferrari, they actively colluded to pool their prize money for race wins while excluding the team's other regular driver, Luigi Musso.

Essentially, racing drivers are hypercompetitive, and self-confidence is a must. If they get beaten, it must be the car's fault. But how to rationalize when they're beaten by someone driving an identical car?

This is the root of many of the great antagonisms through history. It doesn't matter whether one driver *isn't* being given preferential treatment if the other one genuinely believes that they are. And, of course, even given modern production techniques, no two cars are completely identical.

As Fiamma Breschi, Musso's girlfriend and Enzo Ferrari's mistress, put it delightfully in an interview with *The Guardian*: "They used to say that all the cars were prepared in the same way, and perhaps that was true, but as with cakes, there are those that rise more and those that rise less, and the cake that rises more tends to be given to the most greedy."

GLOSSARY

PERALTADA

This very fast and dangerous corner at the Autodromo Hermanos Rodriguez in Mexico City is taken at great speed. Home hero Ricardo Rodriguez was killed there in 1962 when his car's suspension failed, and Ayrton Senna flipped his McLaren in 1991, narrowly escaping serious injury. It has been partially bypassed since the track returned to the F1 calendar in 2015.

'SPYGATE'

In 2007, it was revealed that McLaren chief designer Mike Coughlan had received stolen intellectual property from a disgruntled Ferrari employee, Nigel Stepney. They appear have planned to approach another team for work and use the stolen designs to enhance their credibility once in the job.

Over the course of several months, McLaren were attacked from all sides as the FIA probed who knew what and when they knew it. Although it could not be proven that the data had influenced McLaren's designs, the FIA fined the team $100 million and struck off their constructors' championship points. They also forensically examined the design of the 2008 car for traces of Ferrari intellectual property. Nothing was found.

TEAM ORDERS

A controversial subject, team orders have even been banned (between 2002 and 2010) for having a stifling effect on competition. In effect, the team makes a call to their drivers—either before or during the race—to behave in a certain way. During the 1950s, it was common for a team's lead driver to take over a teammate's car if their own had suffered a technical failure.

There is a rich history of drivers defying such orders—even when in their favor. At the British Grand Prix in 1951, for instance, José Froilán González was leading for Ferrari when he pulled into the pits to let team leader Alberto Ascari take over. Ascari told him he was doing a great job and waved him back out again.

Team orders were theoretically banned after a furor at the Austrian Grand Prix in 2002 when Rubens Barrichello was ordered to move over and let his Ferrari teammate Michael Schumacher win. Arguably, it was Barrichello's grudging and theatrical execution—he waited until the finishing line was in sight—that caused the ruckus.

Ultimately, the FIA had to lift the ban when it proved impossible to police. In 2010, Ferrari—again—used the not-very-coded radio message "Fernando is faster than you" to instruct Felipe Massa to give way to Fernando Alonso.

RACING CIRCUITS

RACING CIRCUITS
STREETS AND AIRSTRIPS

FUN FACT

If you look at Silverstone on Google Earth, the old runways are still clearly visible.

HISTORICAL TIDBIT

Only one street race has survived the test of time in F1: the Monaco Grand Prix. First held in 1929, it has been part of the F1 season every year since the world championship began in 1950.

KEY PERSON

According to popular belief, Maurice Geoghegan is the person who organized the first unofficial race at Silverstone, sneaking in with a group of like-minded friends with sports cars in 1946.

The first organized motor races followed smartly on the heels of the invention of the motor car. The question was where to hold these events, since no purpose-built facilities existed, and the motor car was still considered a dangerous and unwelcome interloper by other users of the roads.

The first race to carry the Grand Prix name was held in France in 1906, on a 64-mile triangular circuit just east of the city of Le Mans. As an event, it was vastly different from modern Grands Prix: it was held over two days as a timed endurance run, with competitors starting at 90-second intervals, as in a cycling time trial. Although the roads were theoretically closed to other traffic, the scale of the route made this virtually impossible to police.

Practical considerations quickly drove race organizers to formulate shorter routes, causing less disruption—and, perhaps more importantly, enabling them to marshal spectators more effectively and charge them for the privilege of watching. The time-trial format also gave way to elbows-out racing, where all the cars started together.

Still, apart from a few notable exceptions—such as the banked speedbowl at Brooklands in southwest London, England—few permanent motor racing facilities were built in the first half century of motor racing. Since car ownership was still relatively unusual, it made sense to hold events in or near urban centers, which meant racing on the streets.

This began to change post–World War II as mass car ownership grew, and enterprising individuals found creative new uses for airstrips that had been augmented for wartime use. RAF Silverstone in England opened as a training base for bomber pilots in 1943. By 1947, the base had been vacated by the Royal Air Force and questions were being asked in the House of Commons about its future—and about damage caused by vandals and trespassers. Among these illicit visitors were young men racing self-built cars around the disused runways.

Three years later, Silverstone held the first World Championship Formula 1 race.

RACING CIRCUITS
ETERNAL CLASSICS

FUN FACT

Although part of the Nürburgring was redeveloped in the
1980s to create a three-mile
Grand Prix layout compliant
with modern safety standards,
the rest of the postwar track is
still there. You can pay to drive
your road car or motorcycle
on it.

HISTORICAL TIDBIT

Belgian politics, combined with
concerns about safety standards at Spa-Francorchamps,
led to the construction of a new
Belgian Grand Prix venue at
Nivelles, south of Brussels, in
1971. Drivers and spectators hated the track, and it only hosted
the event twice. The location is
now an industrial estate.

KEY PERSON

Three-time world champion
Niki Lauda was almost fatally
burned in an accident at the
Nürburgring in 1976. The previous year, he'd set the F1 lap
record for the 14-mile layout, a
record that stands to this day.

One of the most controversial elements of Formula 1's push into new territories over the past two decades has been the gradual squeezing out of
much-loved events and venues. Only the Monaco Grand Prix, considered the
crown jewel of F1, is believed to be completely safe.

Other classic venues have come under threat, either because they
can't be adapted to suit ever-faster cars, or because they can't afford the
ever-increasing cost of hosting a Grand Prix. Silverstone, famously, has
been treated like a punching bag for many years by Bernie Ecclestone, until
recently the sport's "ringmaster." He once described it as "a country fair
masquerading as a world-class venue."

The key is adaptation for survival. The Belgian Spa-Francorchamps
started life in the prewar era as an ultrafast blast around nine miles of
public roads. It's now a permanent facility, just over four miles long, but
many of the elements that drivers loved remain, including unpredictable
Ardennes weather, high top speeds, and soaring elevation changes. A key
corner is Eau Rouge (literally "red water," since the track crosses a creek
where the iron-rich water runs reddish orange). The track flicks left-right at
the bottom of a steep incline before heading upward again, and for many
years taking it flat-out was considered a rite of passage. It was incredibly
dangerous.

Threat was also the main appeal of the Nürburging in Germany, just
over the border from Spa and suffering the same fickle climate. The original circuit was over 17 miles long and dipped and twisted like a roller
coaster. At a little over 14 miles in its postwar form, it became the main
venue for the German Grand Prix. Drivers loved and feared it in equal measure, and even boycotted the race in 1970. The proximity of the barriers,
with dense forest beyond, magnified the effects of any crash. If the worst
happened, the sheer length of the circuit meant it would be a long time
before help arrived.

FUN FACT

Shanghai International Circuit in China was built in 2003 on reclaimed swampland, stabilized by 40,000 concrete piles and tons of polystyrene.

HISTORICAL TIDBIT

The infrequently held South African Grand Prix went on a long hiatus in the 1980s, during which time the Kyalami circuit was totally redesigned—and became counter-clockwise rather than clockwise. This confused drivers who remembered it from the first time round: Andrea de Cesaris arrived, looked at the course, and said, "They've put the gravel traps in the wrong place."

KEY PERSON

F1's first go-to circuit designer was Hans Hugenholtz, who was responsible for the much-loved Suzuka in Japan as well as Spain's Jarama and Belgium's Zolder (both no longer Grand Prix venues).

The shape of the Formula 1 calendar has been transformed by the sport's expansion into new territories, mostly in the east. Eight of the twenty races on the 2017 schedule are at circuits built since 1999, and two more are "old" venues—in Austria and Mexico—which have been greatly redeveloped.

In our increasingly prosperous but crowded world, building a new circuit demands a great deal of investment, vacant real estate, and political willpower. It's no surprise, then, that many of these venues are bankrolled by governments keen to put their countries on the international sporting map (see chapter 7: Taking Care of Business).

Malaysia set the template for New Model F1 with Sepang International Circuit, which opened in 1999. Designed by architect Hermann Tilke, who went on to become F1's preferred circuit wrangler, and located strategically right next to Kuala Lumpur International Airport, it took a blank-slate approach. Where older circuits tended to follow the lines of public roads or exploited happy accidents of topography, Sepang was carefully designed to offer a variety of straights and corners, with large runoff areas in case of accidents. Spectators were held at a safe distance behind barriers and fencing.

Tilke is a keen amateur racer himself, and his modus operandi is to include sections that are deliberately intended to induce drivers to make mistakes, thereby conjuring opportunities for overtaking. Turns 1-2-3 at Sepang are a prime example of this: a hairpin at the end of a long straight, followed quickly by two more bends of changing radius, and with a slightly off-camber surface in places.

The downside of big, open, wide-track circuits with carefully managed top speeds and acres of runoff is a slightly homogenous look, which partially accounts for Tilke being such a polarizing figure among F1 fans. Those who dislike the new tracks complain that they lack character and don't penalize drivers enough in terms of lap time and track position if they make a mistake and go off.

RACING CIRCUITS
RACING IN THE CITY

FUN FACT

The new street circuit in Baku, Azerbaijan, passes within inches of a UNESCO World Heritage site.

HISTORICAL TIDBIT

The Circuito de Boavista street circuit in Portugal only hosted two World Championship Grands Prix before it fell out of use in the late 1950s. It was revived fifty years later and hosted a small number of World Touring Car Championship rounds.

KEY PERSON

German architect and racing enthusiast Hermann Tilke has played a key role in the design or redevelopment of most races in the F1 calendar.

The easiest way to bring racing to the people, rather than expecting the people to bring themselves to the racing, is to stage events in urban environments. That was how top-class motorsport (largely) rolled during the prewar era, before the advent of permanent circuits and when safety standards were somewhat lacking.

The shift toward permanent facilities began in the 1950s, but many Grands Prix that became regular fixtures in later years started life on the streets. The Spanish Grand Prix, for instance, has been running at the purpose-built Circuit de Catalunya, north of Barcelona, for over twenty-five years—but it was first held in 1951 in the suburb of Pedralbes, then later in Montjuich Park.

Portugal hosted its national race on the streets of Porto, with a layout that featured the harbor front. The Avus circuit in Berlin, a flat-out blast along what was the first highway in Europe with a huge banked corner at one end, took over the German Grand Prix just once, in 1959. The streets of Buenos Aires accommodated the Argentine Grand Prix before a full-time track was built on the outskirts of the city.

Urban landscapes brought their own hazards. Road furniture—including tram lines, cobblestones, and manhole covers—were a lap-by-lap challenge to the unwary, as were the bumps. (To gain FIA Grade 1 status, tracks today must be almost pool-table smooth.) The denizens of the built environment were among the most unpredictable—spectators and their pets would often choose not to let the passage of racing cars put them off trying to cross the road.

Given all this, along with complaints about noise and inconvenience, street circuits have declined in popularity. There are now three on the F1 calendar, all based in places where political will trumps people power: Monaco, Singapore, and Baku, Azerbaijan. Only a fool would move to Monaco and complain about an event that has been running for almost a century.

RACING CIRCUITS
REBORN IN THE USA

FUN FACT

Ferrari is the most successful manufacturer on US soil, with nine wins as of 2016.

HISTORICAL TIDBIT

American racer Harry Schell cheekily took a shortcut in practice for the 1959 US Grand Prix at Sebring, nailing a very good starting position but drawing a furious protest from Enzo Ferrari.

KEY PERSON

Tavo Hellmund was the driving force behind the construction of the Circuit of the Americas in Austin, Texas, though he was the victim of a boardroom coup before it held its first race.

Formula 1's on-off relationship with the United States began in 1950, when motorsport's governing body decided to include the Indianapolis 500 as a points-scoring round of the championship. Thus, Johnnie Parsons became the first US Grand Prix winner without ever setting foot in an F1 car.

For a full decade, this optimistic, hands-across-the-ocean scheme proceeded with very few takers on either side. There was no real attempt to harmonize the regulations to allow IndyCars to race in F1 events and vice versa; if you wanted to contest the full World Championship, you needed to have two types of car. In an era before jet aviation, there was little appetite for it.

Ferrari had a crack in 1952 with Alberto Ascari, but the car wasn't up to the job and the team withdrew to Europe to lick its wounds. Troy Ruttmann, the 1952 Indy winner, crossed the pond a few years later to contest a few Grands Prix in a Maserati, without much success either.

F1 would continue for decades to try entering America, without great success. In 1959, the first "proper" US Grand Prix was held in Sebring, Florida, home of the famous 12-hour sports car race. The US Grand Prix then transferred to Riverside, California, but the race was insufficiently promoted and failed to catch the imagination of the locals.

Since then, US Grands Prix have been held at Watkins Glen, on street circuits in Long Beach, Dallas, Detroit and Phoenix, and even at an unpopular temporary track in the parking area of Caesar's Palace casino, Las Vegas. The event returned to Indianapolis in 2000, using a newly built loop of asphalt on the infield of the legendary oval, but that stopped in 2007.

The US Grand Prix was revived in 2012 on a new circuit in Austin, Texas, and, despite sometimes shaky finances, it's been a great success. The sport's new owners have plans to host at least two more events a year on US soil.

CASUALTIES OF COMMERCE

Hosting a Grand Prix is an expensive business—and, because of escalator clauses built into most contracts, it gets pricier year-on-year. As a result of that, over the years, regional and state governments have gradually replaced private investors as race promoters. Sometimes the money runs out, at other times the political will goes first.

KOREA

A classic white elephant facility, Korea International Circuit was built at great expense and hosted just four F1 events, from 2010 to 2013. The original plan was for it to be the centerpiece of new urban development, in effect a street circuit. But when the local government regime that had pushed the project through were voted out of office, the proposed new city was never built. The track's remote location—by the unremarkable port of Mokpo, 250 miles south of Seoul—attracted few spectators, making the Korean Grand Prix a financial flop.

INDIA

Opened in 2011, if not quite finished—many in the media mocked the "stairway to heaven" in one of the paddock buildings, terminating in midair—the Buddh International Circuit was intended to underpin India's growing reputation as an economic powerhouse. Sadly, it also confirmed many prejudices about doing business with India, especially in terms of the red tape involved. For the teams, getting the cars and equipment through customs proved troublesome, and the promoters became embroiled in a dispute with the regional government over the event's tax status. The Indian Grand Prix went on hiatus in 2014, three years into a five-year contract, and has not returned to the calendar.

TURKEY

Having hosted its first race in 2005, Istanbul Park is considered one of favored F1 track architect Hermann Tilke's finest works. But it lacked public transport links to Istanbul and failed to generate much interest from the soccer-mad local populace. Its state funding ran out in 2011.

GLOSSARY

BARRIERS

Both purpose-built and street tracks require barriers to prevent the cars—or debris—from crossing the circuit boundaries in the event of an accident. In the modern era, steel fences are the boundary of last resort; in corners or other areas of potential danger, there will be a gravel trap or asphalt runoff zone, followed by a deformable wall (often made from stacks of tires) before the barrier. There will also be a number of strategically located gaps to allow rescue vehicles onto the circuit, as well as "windows" for photographers to shoot through.

FIA GRADE 1

Motorsport's governing body gives circuits a rating, based on size, facilities, safety features, and the flatness of the surface. This grade determines what level of racing they can host. Grade 1 status is the highest, and it is a prerequisite for hosting F1 events.

INSPECTION

All tracks must pass an inspection by the FIA's safety director, who will examine not just the quality of the track surface, barriers, and runoff areas, but also the effectiveness of the drainage.

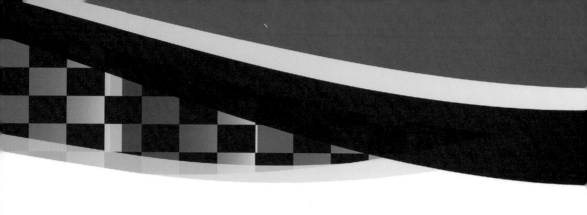

MARSHALS

The first responders to any incident are usually the trackside marshals, mostly volunteer enthusiasts drawn from local motor clubs. Despite being amateurs, they are well trained and highly expert—often new Grands Prix on the calendar will recruit marshals from countries with more established events.

MEDICAL FACILITIES

Circuits hosting Grands Prix must offer a high standard of medical backup, including an on-site medical center capable of stabilizing a patient in case of emergency. A Medevac helicopter must also be present and able to take off at all times during an event.

FINISH

FLAG TO FINISH

FLAG TO FINISH
ANATOMY OF A RACE WEEKEND

FUN FACT

First practice for the Singapore Grand Prix is the only track session of that weekend to be held in daylight.

HISTORICAL TIDBIT

In 1985, the Belgian Grand Prix was cancelled after the practice sessions and rescheduled for later in the year. The track had been resurfaced with a new type of high-grip asphalt that began to break up. After protests from the drivers, the race was called off at 8:00 p.m. on the Saturday.

KEY PERSON

Former race engineer Laurent Mekies is the FIA's recently appointed F1 deputy race director, responsible (among other tasks) for making sure race weekends run smoothly.

Like any good story, a race has a beginning, a middle, and an end. At the close of play, the driver who has covered the most distance in the shortest time is the winner; a checkered flag is waved at them as they cross the finishing line, arms aloft in victory, and they proceed from there to collect their trophy and a bottle of sparkling wine.

This story has an extended prologue, though. The team equipment arrives several days earlier, either via charter jet or by road, depending on how far away from home base the race is. At European rounds, the kit includes vast motorhomes that the teams use as operational hubs for their staff over the weekend. These might require up to five trucks just to carry all the pieces, which are assembled long before the action begins and then stripped and packed once the flag has fallen.

The Thursday before, the race is given over to media time, as journalists, photographers, and TV camera crews from all over the world charge from one interview slot to another in pursuit of a story. Formula 1 might take up just twenty or so of the weekends in a year, but in the age of the Internet its news agenda is a 24/7 monster that demands incessant feeding.

Drivers, naturally, look forward to Friday, when track activity begins with two 90-minute practice sessions. Each team arrives with a plan to make the most of this time; most drivers won't need to learn the circuit, but they do need to cultivate an understanding of how the car behaves in changing conditions. They may try to fine-tune it to find more speed—an F1 car's suspension is much more adjustable than a road car's—but this time is devoted primarily to getting the best out of the tires.

On Saturday, another hour of practice takes place before qualifying begins—a crucial period that determines the starting order for the race.

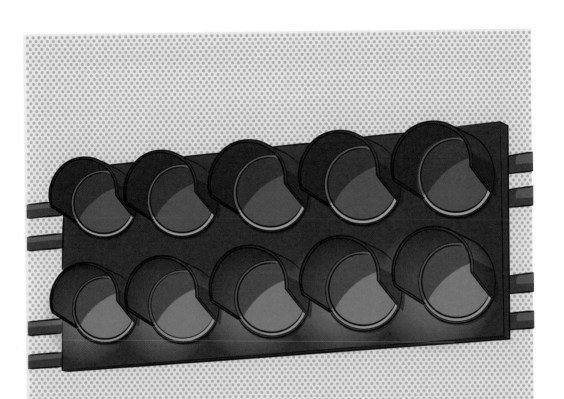

FLAG TO FINISH
QUALIFYING

FUN FACT

Among the shortest-lived changes to the qualifying format—and certainly the most hated—was the "countdown" elimination format introduced at the beginning of the 2016 season. It was dropped after one race.

HISTORICAL TIDBIT

In 2004, all of Saturday's track activities at the Japanese Grand Prix had to be cancelled because of a typhoon passing through the area. Qualifying had to be held early on the Sunday morning.

KEY PERSON

Sebastian Vettel currently holds the record for setting the most pole positions in one season—fifteen in nineteen races, set during the 2011 season.

The all-important process of setting the race's starting order has changed a great deal over the years—even more so in the past couple of decades, as it has become a television spectacle in itself.

The starting grids for prewar events were often determined by drawing lots. But this opened the problem of how to weed out less-than-serious competitors in a transparent and meritocratic way, especially if there were too many entries. Ranking the drivers in order of times set during practice, with the fastest starting at the front (and a cutoff point beyond which the slowest were excluded), was the obvious solution.

In the immediate postwar era, all laps in practice counted, but as F1 evolved as a spectator sport, specific qualifying sessions became part of the crowd-pleasing package. Until 1996, these were split into two sessions—one on Friday, the other on Saturday—with a driver's fastest time overall setting their place in the starting order.

Since then, the qualifying format has been altered regularly, usually with the specific aim of making it must-watch television. The challenge here is that the perfect qualifying lap is an individual feat, best accomplished when no other cars are around to get in the way.

There have been plenty of false steps and reversions, but the present setup has been relatively stable since 2006. The single qualifying session is now split into three phases. In the first, which lasts 18 minutes, all twenty drivers have to set a time, and at the end of it the five slowest are eliminated. In the second, which lasts 15 minutes, the remaining drivers run again and then the slowest five are dropped, leaving ten to contest the final 10 minutes.

A tactical wrinkle here is that everyone who makes it through to the final stage must start the race on the set of tires they used to set their quickest time in the second phase. Everyone else gets a free choice.

FLAG TO FINISH
STARTING

Sensors in the track surface automatically detect anyone moving before the lights go out.

HISTORICAL TIDBIT

One of the worst false starts in F1 history was at Monza in 1978. It resulted in the death of Lotus driver Ronnie Peterson, and it was caused by human error. The starter gave the signal to go before the entire field had lined up on the grid, leading to a huge crash at the first corner.

KEY PERSON

Former Brabham mechanic Charlie Whiting is the FIA's race director and safety delegate. He is responsible for activating the start procedure at every Grand Prix.

As the seconds tick past before the race starts, a driver's heart rate can spike to over 180 beats per minute. The stakes are high: a mistake at this point might scupper any good work done in qualifying, or cause a crash that could put the driver out of the race. A great deal of energy is about to be unleashed.

The work begins several minutes before the start itself, as the drivers work through a very specific set of procedures to get ready for the off. Having parked on the grid in qualifying order, the whole field undertakes a formation lap; this gives them the opportunity to work some heat into the tires and adjust the various electronic settings on the steering wheel, ensuring the car itself is set up for the start. Although traction and launch control systems are banned, engine modes are available to give power and torque delivery that will suit a getaway from a standing start.

Likewise, a rule introduced in 2016 banning twin-clutch systems put more of the onus on the drivers to get the start right.

From a booth overlooking the grid, the FIA's race director decides when the drivers are ready and manually activates the final part of the start procedure on his console. This illuminates one by one a set of five red lights on a gantry facing the drivers. And then, after a short but randomly determined pause, the control mechanism extinguishes the lights all at once. This is the signal to go.

In the cockpit, the driver has been holding his foot on the accelerator to keep the engine running at the optimum number of revs. It's up to him to react as quickly as possible as the lights go out, then balance clutch and throttle to get as much go-forward as possible without spinning the wheels.

The next thing to worry about is when to brake for the first corner.

FUN FACT

Refueling used to determine the length of a pit stop. Since it was banned, pit crews have turned to a combination of technology and sport science to speed up the wheel-change process. The official pit stop record, held jointly by the Red Bull and Williams teams, is 1.92 seconds.

HISTORICAL TIDBIT

Lewis Hamilton moved from McLaren to Mercedes for the 2013 season, but suffered a brief moment of brain fade during the Chinese Grand Prix and pulled up in the McLaren pit box. The bemused mechanics waved him on.

KEY PERSON

Ross Brawn was the technical director of the Benetton team when refueling was introduced in 1994. He caught on to the idea of the "undercut" much faster than his rivals, sometimes putting less fuel in for a shorter, faster pit stop.

You *could* run an entire Formula 1 race without any of the drivers making a pit stop. The cars don't have to refuel anymore, and it would be easy to make tires that last a full Grand Prix distance.

Strategy makes the racing more interesting, though, which is why the tires are specially designed to offer a range of tradeoffs between grip and lifespan.

The basic strategic play in F1 is called the "undercut." Here you look to overtake the car ahead by pitting first, then using your fresh tires to set a series of fast laps. This means that, when your rival makes his own stop, he'll emerge behind you.

Sound easy? Well, going as fast as possible after your stop depends on leaving the pits with a clear track ahead. Getting stuck behind a slower car will spoil the strategy, so teams monitor all the cars via GPS to get a picture of who will be where at the crucial moment.

Tire choice—how many of each type you bring and when you use them—adds an extra layer of complication and is the key to an effective strategy. Pirelli, F1's sole tire supplier, offers a family of five dry-weather rubber compounds: ultra-soft, super-soft, soft, medium, and hard.

In theory, the softest tires offer the most grip but have the shortest life, while hard tires last longer but provide less grip. Pirelli nominates three types for every circuit, and then the teams have to choose how many of each they want, out of a maximum of thirteen sets per driver, which must last them the whole weekend.

In a dry race, each driver must use at least two different tire compounds, which means making at least one pit stop. How many they actually make is up to them: the speed gain from softer rubber might outweigh the time lost through making more pit stops.

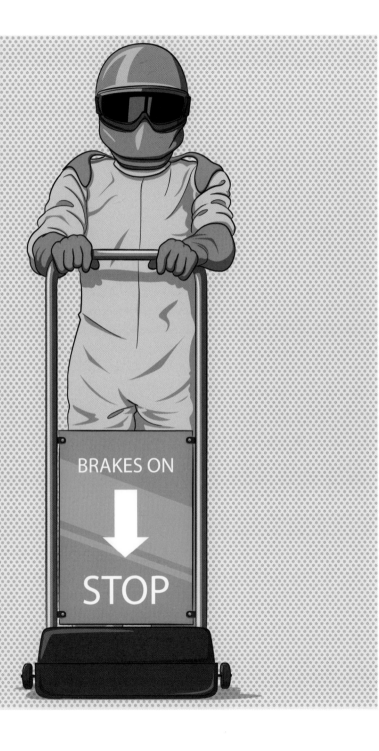

FLAG TO FINISH
KEEPING SCORE

FUN FACT

Because of the dropped-score system of the time—only the best six results counted—Jim Clark scored the maximum possible points when he won the title for Lotus in 1963 and 1965. He actually won seven races in 1963.

HISTORICAL TIDBIT

In a misguided attempt to raise the stakes, double points were awarded in the final race of the 2014 season, the Abu Dhabi Grand Prix. Purists hated the idea. Fortunately, it didn't influence the outcome of the title chase: race winner Lewis Hamilton would have been the champion with or without double points.

KEY PERSON

As F1's "ringmaster" until early 2017, Bernie Ecclestone has been the driving force behind most of the changes to the scoring system since 1991.

Even after nearly seventy years, the Formula 1 World Championship's scoring system remains a work in progress. But it's a lot simpler than it used to be.

Unlike, say, NASCAR, where points are awarded all the way down to the minor placings, it's been a key principle in F1 from the start that points should be valuable and hard to obtain.

From 1950 to 1959, points were awarded from first to fifth place. That number has gradually increased, albeit at a glacial pace—the top ten now get points on a scale of 25-18-15-12-10-8-6-4-3-2-1, but only since 2010.

As with so many of the changes made to the sporting side of F1, television, commerce, and technology have been the key motivators here. The modern system has to be transparent, easy to calculate, and readily understood by viewers. It also has to provide an incentive to push hard for the best results rather than stealthily banking points. Ideally, so as not to leave the last few races as dead rubbers, the championship should go right down to the wire.

Since 1991, the result of every race has counted toward both the drivers' and the constructors' championships. Before then, various dropped-score systems prevailed, in which only a certain number of a driver's best results counted toward the final tally. For a few years, there was even a point awarded for setting the fastest lap.

A certain logic applied here: in the early years of the championship, there was no guarantee that every driver or team would or could participate in every round, and cars were far less reliable than they are today. Now the teams are contractually obligated to run at every round or risk being booted out of the championship entirely.

Pos	No	Driver	Constructor	Laps	Time/Retired	Points
1	44	Lewis Hamilton	Mercedes	70	1:31:05.296	25
2	5	Sebastian Vettel	Ferrari	70		18
3	77	Valtteri Bottas	Williams Mercedes	70		15
4	33	Max Verstappen	Red Bull Racing	70		
5	6	Nico Rosberg	Mercedes	70	+62.093s	
6	7	Kimi Räikkönen	Ferrari	70	+63.012s	
7	3	Daniel Ricciardo	Red Bull Racing	69	+63.634s	
8	27	Nico Hulkenberg	Force India	69	+1 lap	
9	55	Carlos Sainz	Toro Rosso Ferrari	69	+1 lap	
10	11	Sergio Perez	Force India	69	+1 lap	
11	14	Fernando Alonso	McLaren Honda	69	+1 lap	
12	26	Daniil Kvyat	Toro Rosso Ferrari	68	+2 laps	
13	21	Esteban Gutierrez	Haas Ferrari	68	+2 laps	
14	8	Romain Grosjean	Haas Ferrari	68	+2 laps	
15	9	Marcus Ericsson	Sauber Ferrari	68	+2 laps	
16	20	Kevin Magnussen	Renault	68	+2 laps	
17	94	Pascal Wehrlein	MRT Mercedes	68	+2 laps	
18	12	Felipe Nasr	Sauber Ferrari	68	+2 laps	
19	88	Rio Haryanto	MRT Mercedes	35		
NC	19	Felipe Massa	Williams Mercedes	16	DNF	
NC	30	Jolyon Palmer	Renault	9	DNF	
NC	22	Jenson Button	McLaren Honda		DNF	

FLAG TO FINISH
MANUFACTURERS' vs. DRIVERS' CHAMPIONSHIPS

FUN FACT

You might imagine that, every year, the champion driver would be in a car made by the champion constructor, but on ten occasions they haven't.

HISTORICAL TIDBIT

McLaren hammered Ferrari by 143.5 points to 57.5 in the 1984 constructors' standings, but the McLaren drivers—Niki Lauda and Alain Prost—were separated by the narrowest margin of all time: half a point. Prost missed out because the Monaco Grand Prix, which he won, was stopped early because of rain, and half points were awarded.

KEY PERSON

The late Enzo Ferrari's eponymous team is the most successful of all time, with sixteen Constructors' Championships at the time of writing.

Which of the two titles is the most significant? The answer depends on who you ask.

To most F1 fans, it's not a question at all. The drivers' title is the most important and that's that. You could argue, too, that the wider world shares this point of view: when you hear about the result of a race on the news, the name of the driver usually leads. The identity of the constructor is only cited to lend context and is rarely treated as something of interest in itself.

Some fans follow teams rather than drivers—perhaps the price of merchandise is partly to blame for that. For the most part, though, the human factor trumps the mechanical in the affections of the masses.

Commercially, the constructors' title assumes a far greater significance, and it can make or break careers. The trophy was first awarded in 1958 as part of a concerted effort to charm teams and manufacturers into a formula that had endured a shaky start. The first two years of the championship had been dominated by prewar machinery, and the dearth of new F1 cars led to it being open only to Formula 2 cars in 1952 and 1953. New engine rules from 1954 on stimulated interest, but F1 was still a sticky commercial pitch for years after that.

More pressingly, in the modern era a team's position in the constructors' standings at the end of the year determines their share of the prize pot. This unlocks revenues worth tens of millions of dollars—so, if you were to ask a team principal which of the two championships is the most significant . . .

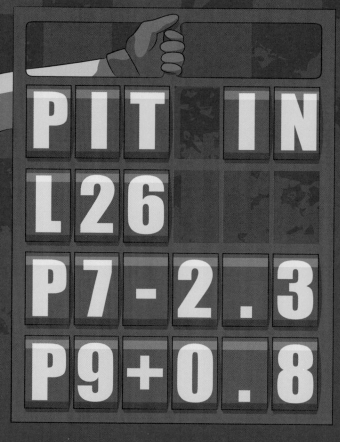

THE APPLIANCE OF SCIENCE

Picking the right moment to make a pit stop isn't a matter of guesswork. In effect, when a driver comes into the pits, he is giving up track position. For this reason, teams have to keep an eye on which cars are ahead of their drivers, especially backmarkers who might slow them down either before or after the stop. Any delay could prove costly—the outcome of the 2017 Australian Grand Prix was decided when Lewis Hamilton pitted from the lead and then emerged behind Max Verstappen, who held him up for several laps. Hamilton eventually finished second.

Teams have evolved sophisticated strategic tools to help them track their own performance, measure it in real time against what their opponents are doing, and then use that intelligence proactively to make decisions that can shape the outcome of the race. The key to success here is the tradeoff between richness and simplicity: a race is a constantly changing environment, and team strategists must be able to absorb both the big picture and the granular detail at a glance.

This technology has great potential in other fields. The McLaren team, for instance, has been working with London's Heathrow airport to adapt their race strategy tools into a system that can help air and ground traffic controllers optimize the flow of aircraft.

GLOSSARY

DEGRADATION

On your road car, you generally change your tires when—or shortly before—the outer layer of rubber wears out. F1 tires rarely reach this point. When drivers and engineers talk about "degradation," they mean that the tire has lost its ability at the chemical level to grip the track surface. As a rule of thumb, the softer the rubber compound, the more chemical grip it offers, but the quicker it loses that grip—while still having plenty of material left on the outer casing.

PIT STOPS

Both an essential process and a tactical move, a pit stop represents the peak of team activity: getting it right demands perfect synchronization between the driver and his pit crew, and the right calls from the engineers on the pit wall. For safety, the pit lane is segregated from the main part of the circuit and is subject to a speed limit.

PRACTICE

Each Grand Prix weekend features three practice sessions in which teams and drivers try to perfect their cars' mechanical setup and get a feel for how the tires will behave in the race. Drivers spend so much time on simulators in the modern era that there is no need to "learn" the circuit as such, even for rookies.

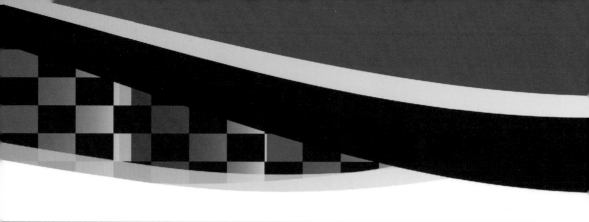

REFUELING

Stopping for fuel has been an irregular feature of F1 since the World Championship began in 1950s. Until the 1980s, it was very low tech—basically tipping a churn of petrol into the fuel tank via a funnel. It was outlawed in the 1980s after a number of incidents (including Nigel Mansell suffering chemical burns to his testicles after a spill), then reintroduced from 1994 to 2009, using a similar technology to aircraft refueling.

TELEMETRY

Data gathered from the many sensors measuring cars' behavior is transmitted wirelessly to the teams, a process referred to as telemetry.

UNDERCUT

A strategic move in which a driver passes another without actually overtaking the opponent on the track, undercutting usually involves pitting first and then going faster before the other driver makes his pit stop.

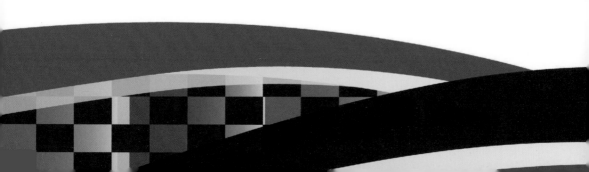

STAYING ALIVE

STAYING ALIVE
STRAW BALES AND CLOTH CAPS

FUN FACT

In the early days of the Silverstone circuit, the corners on the former airfield were marked out with oil barrels—into which competitors regularly crashed.

HISTORICAL TIDBIT

Hans Herrman inadvertently held back the cause of F1 safety after his spectacular crash in the 1959 German Grand Prix. A photo of him crouching on the asphalt as his BRM cartwheeled away galvanized arguments against seat belts.

KEY PERSON

It only became compulsory to wear a hardhat in 1952, after the death of veteran driver Luigi Fagioli in a sports car race in Monaco.

Our civilization's attitude to managing risk has altered dramatically over the past century. The first motor races were held on public roads that weren't even closed to other traffic for the occasion. A series of unconnected accidents on the 1903 Paris-Madrid road race put paid to that, but even after motor racing became better organized, safety standards were still lax.

Part of this can be put down to lack of relevant technology, but much of it was cultural, this being an era when it was still possible for tobacco companies to advertise the health benefits of smoking, for instance. When the Formula 1 World Championship began in 1950, racing drivers wore simple overalls while on the job—flame-retardant fabrics lay in the future—and crash helmets were a mildly controversial topic. Some drivers continued to use cloth caps, like those worn by fighter pilots, rather than helmets; until 1952 there was no obligation to wear head protection (not that the cork-lined tin hats of the day would have offered much).

"When I started, my father wanted me to wear a helmet," says Stirling Moss. "I said, 'But, Dad, that's a bit sissy.'"

Mislaid machismo would get in the way of safety development for the next two decades. Race promoters also had a vested interest in minimal safety provisions at racetracks because improved standards came at a cost, and few people were asking for them, anyway. It was easy and cheap to place bales of straw around track boundaries to absorb hits from cars and drivers; unlike today, there was no requirement for vehicle bodies to deform progressively in impacts, and drivers didn't wear seat belts. In fact, it was considered better to be thrown out of a car during an accident than to be trapped in it afterward if it caught fire.

STAYING ALIVE
FIGHTING FIRES

FUN FACT

Modern F1 car fuel tanks are made of rubber and Kevlar, and must be puncture-proof to a pressure of 400 pounds.

HISTORICAL TIDBIT

When Niki Lauda crashed at the Nürburgring in 1976 and was trapped in his burning car, the nearest fire marshal was too far away. Other competitors—Arturo Merzario, Guy Edwards, Brett Lunger, and Harald Ertl—stopped and rescued him from the flames.

KEY PERSON

Elio de Angelis was the last F1 driver to die as a result of fire. He crashed during a test at Paul Ricard in the south of France in 1986.

Drivers who showed little fear of injury or death in an accident still dreaded one thing in particular: fire. Here death would not be instant, but painful and lingering. Most drivers of the 1950s and 1960s cited the possibility of becoming trapped in a car that had caught fire as a very good reason to avoid wearing a seat belt.

Cars in this era were little more than bombs on wheels, often built with exotic, lightweight metals such as magnesium (which gives off intense heat when it burns) and carrying unprotected fuel tanks stuffed with high-octane juice. In an accident, spilled fuel was likely, with inevitable consequences when it came into contact with a heat source or spark. A crashed car might come to rest against one of the straw bales that marked the outer edges of circuits of the day, barriers that were highly flammable when dry.

Until the 1970s, firefighting equipment was sparsely deployed around race circuits, and often left in the hands of untrained volunteers rather than professional firefighters. The results were predictably catastrophic. When Lorenzo Bandini crashed at the chicane on the Monaco harbor front in 1967, his Ferrari came to rest upside down on top of straw bales. He was trapped inside as a broken fuel pipe created an inferno that the marshals nearby, with inadequate fire extinguishers and no fireproof clothing, struggled to extinguish. A TV helicopter hovering above fanned the flames. Bandini died three days later.

Very little changed in the aftermath. A year later, Jo Schlesser was killed when his magnesium-bodied Honda crashed and burst into flames at Rouen, France. Again, the water-based fire-extinguishing equipment wasn't up to the task: the burning remnants of the car floated on the water, creating rivers of fire.

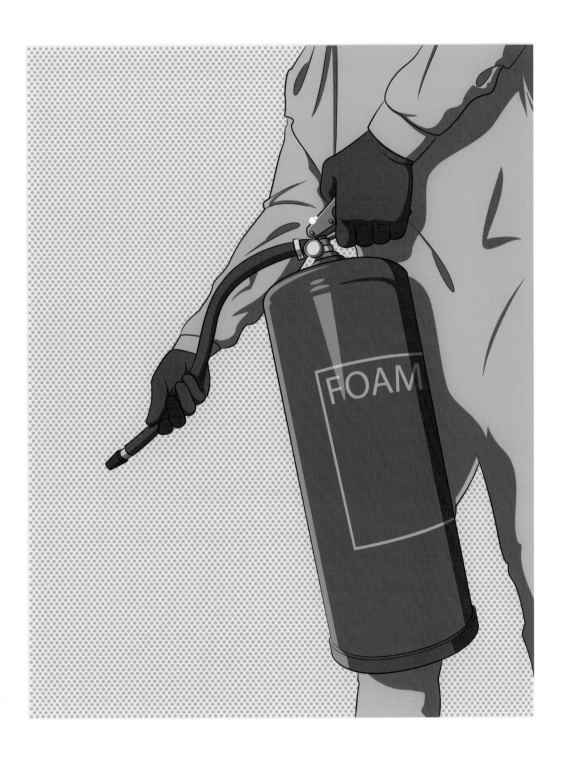

STAYING ALIVE
STEWART STANDS UP

FUN FACT

Jackie Stewart was also skilled with a gun, narrowly missing out on selection for the British Olympic shooting team in 1960.

HISTORICAL TIDBIT

After Stewart's safety campaign, many circuits (grudgingly) installed Armco barriers. These weren't always maintained well: in 1975, mechanics from the race teams had to be drafted in to mend rusting Armco mountings at Montjuic Park, home of the Spanish Grand Prix.

KEY PERSON

The Grand Prix Drivers' Association (GPDA) was a relatively toothless body until Stewart took over in the late 1960s, but it was triple world champion Jack Brabham who swung the other members in favor of the crucial boycott of the Nürburgring in 1970.

One driver can take most of the credit for starting a revolution in Formula 1 safety: Jackie Stewart. His campaign to improve standards brought him into direct conflict not only with race promoters and other vested interests, but also with so-called experts and even his own colleagues.

Over nine seasons in F1, he won the World Championship three times. Even before he won his first in 1969, though, he was beginning to agitate for better driver welfare. The trigger came in 1966, when eight of the fifteen drivers who started the Belgian Grand Prix—Stewart among them—crashed on the opening lap when a sudden downpour soaked the track surface.

Stewart was travelling at upwards of 160 miles per hour as he speared off the track, into a telephone pole. Two other drivers stopped and had to borrow a toolkit from a spectator to remove Stewart's steering wheel and free him from the cockpit. He regained consciousness on the floor of what he later referred to as "the so-called medical center." It was dirty and strewn with cigarette butts. His ambulance then got lost on the way to the hospital.

After recovering, Stewart began bringing his own doctor to race weekends—an innovation that attracted much ridicule. Mirth turned to anger in some quarters as Stewart pushed on, demanding that circuits install proper safety barriers and better runoff areas, and that seat belts and full-face crash helmets become compulsory.

With the help of some key allies in the driving fraternity, Stewart even managed to arrange boycotts of some circuits against entrenched opposition from within the sport. Slowly, he managed to engineer a change in racing's culture: no longer would injury or death be considered acceptable risk.

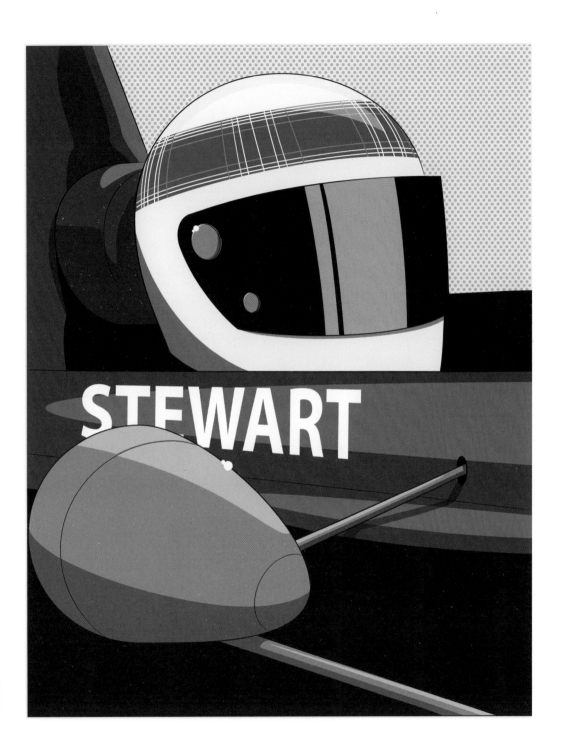

STAYING ALIVE
DOCTORS IN THE HOUSE

FUN FACT

In case of failure, the FIA brings two of the 550-bhp Mercedes-AMG medical cars to each Grand Prix.

HISTORICAL TIDBIT

In 2002, there was a freak accident during the Brazilian Grand Prix weekend. The medical car was attending a crash involving local driver Enrique Bernoldi when another F1 car smashed into it.

KEY PERSON

Dr. Ian Roberts is currently the FIA's rescue coordinator and the medical car's permanent resident, along with driver Alan van der Merwe. There will often be a third passenger, usually a local doctor.

The catalyst for the next big change in Formula 1 safety was an accident at the beginning of the 1978 Italian Grand Prix that claimed the life of Lotus driver Ronnie Peterson. In spite of the improvements happening elsewhere, medical facilities and coverage at circuits remained primitive. (Before his retirement in 1973, Jackie Stewart had complained that the on-site doctor at one track was a gynecologist rather than one with a relevant qualification.)

This was already changing when Peterson met his unfortunate end. Brabham team owner Bernie Ecclestone, a man increasingly involved in the running of the sport and pushing for more influence, had invited a qualified neurosurgeon to consult on possible improvements. Professor Sid Watkins duly found himself in the thick of it at Monza, where there was no car to get him to the scene of Peterson's accident, and—after he'd made his way there on foot—he was turned away by police. The semi-conscious Peterson had to be lifted through the chaotic rabble to a helicopter because there was no ambulance. He died later in the hospital.

In the late 1970s, Ecclestone was in the process of, in effect, unionizing the teams with himself at the head. In the teeth of opposition from vested interests who saw no value in spending money on better medical care, he empowered Watkins to push for—and receive—a minimum standard for on-site medical centers, qualified doctors, and a medical evacuation helicopter for every race. Just as significantly, he pioneered the idea of the medical car—not an ambulance, but a high-powered road car driven by a skilled ex-racer and carrying emergency stabilization equipment, along with a doctor. For many years, this was Watkins, the neurosurgeon.

Today, the medical car is a Mercedes-AMG C 63 S. It follows the field around for the first lap of the race so that it can arrive at an accident site within seconds.

STAYING ALIVE
DEATH AT IMOLA

FUN FACT

At the time of writing, San Marino 1994 was the last race in which an Italian driver scored points for Ferrari. Nicola Larini finished third.

HISTORICAL TIDBIT

After a number of safety alterations, including the replacement of the Tamburello with a slower left-right-left sweep, the Autodromo Enzo e Dino Ferrari at Imola returned to the calendar in 1995. The San Marino Grand Prix remained in place until 2006.

KEY PERSON

Senna's death led to the reformation of the Grand Prix Drivers' Association after a twelve-year hiatus. Since 2014, the chairman has been a retired F1 driver, Alexander Wurz.

If ever there were such a thing as a cursed weekend, the 1994 San Marino Grand Prix aptly fits that description. Five serious incidents, two of which resulted in fatalities, would have grabbed the world's attention—even if one of those tragic deaths had not been Ayrton Senna, one of the greatest drivers of all time. The loss of Senna almost brought the sport to its knees.

The weekend began with a frightening accident during Friday practice in which Senna's countryman, Rubens Barrichello, narrowly escaped serious injury after his car launched off a curb at high speed and almost vaulted the barriers into a spectator enclosure. If anything, though, this incident served to magnify the complacency that had been growing within F1: Barrichello's survival was taken as evidence of the reassuring strength of modern cars.

The following day, Austrian Roland Ratzenberger was killed when his front wing came loose, also at high speed, and lodged under his car. Unable to brake or steer effectively, he slammed into a concrete wall.

This incident affected Senna deeply. Professor Sid Watkins wrote in his autobiography that Senna cried on his shoulder, but refused to quit the sport, saying, "Sid, there are certain things over which we have no control. I cannot quit—I have to go on."

Senna had been riled by suspicions that Michael Schumacher's Benetton team had been using illegal traction control systems and was determined to beat them. He started the race from pole position and took the lead, but the race had to be neutralized briefly behind the safety car because of another accident. After the race restarted, Senna tore off into the lead again, but one lap later his car left the road at the Tamburello corner, barely slowing from 190 miles per hour as it ran over the grass and into a wall.

The race continued as Senna was airlifted to the hospital, where he was pronounced dead. Later, four mechanics were injured in the pit lane by a loose wheel. F1's complacency had been shattered.

STAYING ALIVE
RETHINKING CAR DESIGN

FUN FACT

The success of the revised F1 crash regulations led the FIA to support the Euro New Car Assessment Program (NCAP) tests that rate road car safety performance, beginning in 1996. These have saved thousands of lives in road accidents.

HISTORICAL TIDBIT

The safety car had already been officially reintroduced during 1993, but the specific car varied from circuit to circuit. Since 1996, as part of a promotional agreement, they have always been high-performance Mercedes.

KEY PERSON

Max Mosley was the FIA president at the time of Senna's death. He played a key role in pushing through safety improvements in the following years, often facing entrenched opposition.

The events of the 1994 San Marino Grand Prix prompted a far-reaching rethink by motor racing's governing body, the FIA. There were a number of short-term solutions put in place so that F1 could continue, such as the installation of temporary chicanes at some circuits during 1994 to reduce speeds in potential danger spots.

Looking forward, the FIA resolved to demand that circuits install bigger runoff areas and more impact-absorbent barriers, along with better catch fencing to protect spectators (several people had suffered minor injuries when debris from the starting line accident at Imola went into a spectator enclosure). Another key focus was on car design, aiming to reduce top speeds and to give drivers better protection in an accident.

The precise cause of Senna's death was put down to a broken suspension wishbone penetrating his crash helmet. Barrichello had broken his nose in his accident, and his head had slammed against the side of the cockpit. At the subsequent Monaco Grand Prix, another driver, Karl Wendlinger, also suffered head injuries in a side-on impact with a crash barrier.

Over the following seasons, the FIA rolled out new crash-testing regulations that required the chassis "tub" to act as a safety cell for drivers. It mandated that the cockpit sides around the head area be higher, made from a deformable padding, and easily removable for quicker driver extraction in case of accidents. In later years, the HANS device (see this chapter's glossary) became mandatory.

Engine sizes were cut—from 3.5-liter V-10s to 3.0 in 1995, then to 2.4 V-8s in 2006. Wheel tethers became compulsory to prevent them becoming detached in an accident, and "unsafe release" penalties were added to the rules governing pit lane activities.

The outside of the cars changed, too, owing to new regulations limiting wing sizes and other bodywork dimensions. From 1998, the tires had to feature grooves to reduce their surface area, but this proved a step too far: "slicks" returned in 2009.

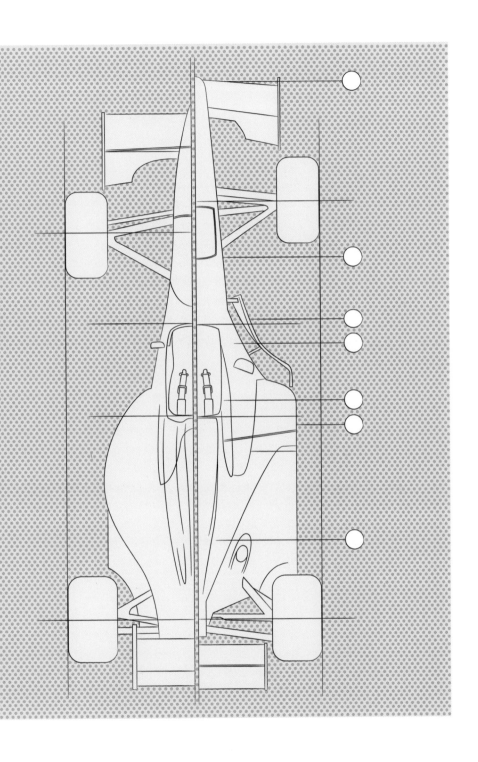

STAYING ALIVE
MODERN SAFETY GEAR

FUN FACT

In the late 1990s, the FIA explored the possibility of fitting airbags to F1 cockpits. After extensive testing, though, the governing body embraced the HANS device instead.

HISTORICAL TIDBIT

Polish driver Robert Kubica was subject to forces 28 times that of gravity when he barrel-rolled his BMW at the 2007 Canadian Grand Prix. He was bruised badly enough to miss the following race, but otherwise unharmed—and won in Canada the following season.

KEY PERSON

The late Jules Bianchi prompted the most recent round of safety improvements, including the "virtual" safety car and the trials of the halo device, when he crashed during the Japanese Grand Prix in 2014.

Rapid advances in fabric technology over the past half century have transformed the look, feel, and effectiveness of safety gear. Fire-retardant driver overalls were compulsory from 1963, but, unlike other measures such as seat belts and helmets, these were more rapidly embraced by drivers, given their aversion to fire.

Still, early fabrics weren't as effective as they could have been, especially in single-layer clothing. In 1975, the FIA defined a minimum standard for fireproof clothing; this, together with the adoption of properly resilient materials such as Nomex, finally banished the placebo effect.

The multilayer suits of the day were heavy, though, and since the 1970s race suit manufacturers have concentrated on reducing bulk and weight while continuing to improve fire resistance. Pit crews, having been allowed to work in shorts and T-shirts up until the 1980s, must now operate in the same gear as the drivers.

The cockpit is a much safer environment than it was, thanks to the adoption of the HANS head restraint to complement the body harnesses. Seat belts were only made mandatory in 1972, and in the modern era are governed by specific rules: they're now six-point harnesses with a single "catch" at the center, enabling the driver to undo it with a single hand movement.

Above the driver's head, the roll cage has to meet impact requirements every bit as strict as those governing frontal, rear, and side impacts. The seat is designed to be removable, and the cockpit sides are reinforced with bulletproof Zylon material.

Although drivers are safer than ever before, it's impossible to neutralize all risks. Work is presently under way on a new form of cockpit protection to shield drivers' heads from flying objects, but the exact form of this has yet to be determined.

EVOLUTION OF THE CRASH HELMET

Wearing a crash helmet only became compulsory in F1 after the death of Luigi Fagioli in 1952, but the cork-lined, hard-shell helmets of the day offered only rudimentary protection—probably not much better than the leather caps they replaced.

What many drivers also failed to realize, even as they made the transition, was that the combination of noise from the engine and that of the wind whistling around their ears was very damaging to their hearing. Most combined an open-faced helmet with goggles, which protected their eyes but not much else. During the Belgian Grand Prix in 1960, Alan Stacey was killed after a bird flew into his face, knocking him unconscious.

Full-face helmets arrived in motorcycle racing first during the 1960s, and then US racer Dan Gurney introduced the idea to F1 at the German Grand Prix in 1968. Take-up was patchy until Lotus driver Jochen Rindt broke his nose in a crash in Spain; this persuaded him to use a full-face helmet. He briefly abandoned it after finding it too hot, only to be hit in the face by a stone during the French Grand Prix in 1970.

Full-face designs are now mandatory, and they must undergo a demanding test regime before being approved for use. A modern F1 helmet is a far cry from the polycarbonate ones of the 1970s: the outer shell is made from carbon fiber, while the inner layers are interleaved with flame-resistant aramid. The visor also has to pass impact tests and, since 2011, it has featured a Zylon strip.

GLOSSARY

ARMCO

A type of crash barrier made from curved metal sheets attached to posts, the Armco functions like a fence. The idea is to absorb or deflect impacts more progressively than other roadside furniture, such as trees.

CATCH FENCING

Abandoned during the 1970s, catch fencing was designed to act as a safety net, progressively slowing cars down if they left the track. In practice it proved indifferently effective and often trapped cars and drivers.

GPDA

Reformed in the aftermath of Ayrton Senna's death in 1994 following a long hiatus, the Grand Prix Drivers' Association was originally formed in 1961 to represent the interests of drivers. At first, it was a fairly passive organization, later energized by Jackie Stewart as a force for change on safety matters during the 1970s.

HALO

Throughout 2016 this new cockpit-protection device was tested during Grand Prix practice sessions. Opinions differed as to its effectiveness and its effects on forward vision.

HANS

The head and neck support device was pioneered in America in the 1980s. Essentially a carbon-fiber frame that rests on the driver's pectoral area and attaches to the crash helmet, it reduces whiplash during impacts. It has been mandatory in F1 since 2003.

RUNOFF AREAS

Introduced as a buffer area in which cars can slow down before they hit anything if they leave the track, a runoff area can take the form of gravel beds or high-grip asphalt. The latter is considered preferable, since cars can become stuck in gravel.

SAFER BARRIER

Steel and foam energy reduction barriers are a more effective solution to trackside safety than Armco, and were first used in oval racing in America. A combination of steel and polystyrene, they deform progressively in impacts.

SAFETY CAR

If a race has to be neutralized because of an incident, the safety car leads the field around at a set pace until the situation has been resolved. Drivers may not overtake one another while running behind it.

UNSAFE RELEASE

Teams that release their car into the path of another in the pit lane, or who fail to attach all the wheels properly during a pit stop, are punished harshly.

VIRTUAL SAFETY CAR

For minor incidents or if action has to be taken quickly, rather than scrambling the safety car, the race director can declare "virtual" safety car conditions. Drivers cannot overtake one another and must stick to an electronically monitored speed limit.

YELLOW FLAGS

Waved by trackside marshals (and displayed to drivers via illuminated signs) to signify danger ahead, a yellow flag indicates that drivers must slow down and not overtake until they pass a green flag, indicating the danger is over.

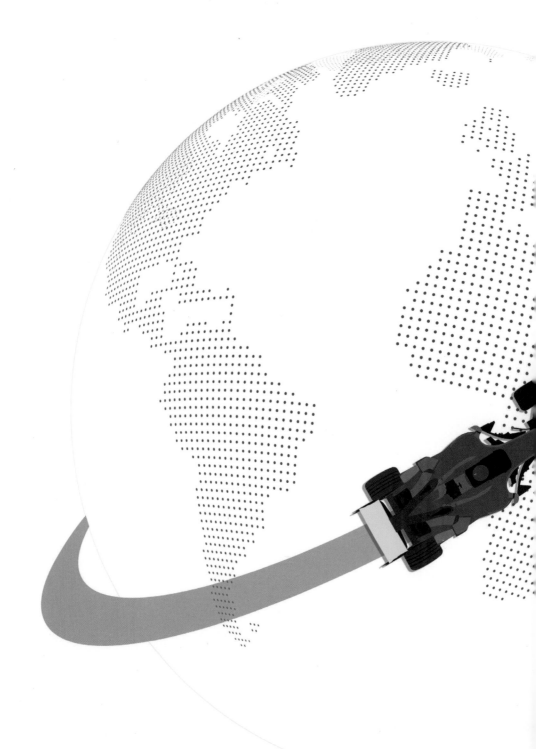

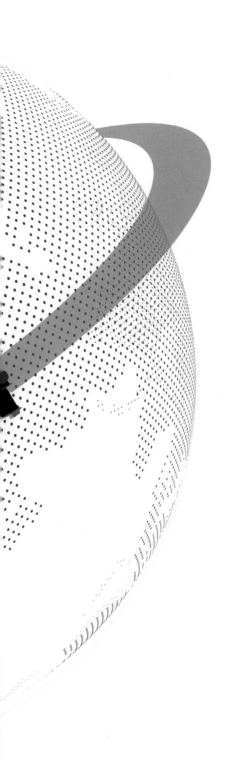

TAKING CARE OF BUSINESS

TAKING CARE OF BUSINESS
THE FIRST MANUFACTURER ERA

FUN FACT

Ferrari already had a competitive F2 car and walked the 1952–1953 seasons. Alberto Ascari's record of consecutive wins in those years stood until Sebastian Vettel broke it in 2013.

HISTORICAL TIDBIT

A non-championship F1 race in Turin in April 1952 was the tipping point for the sport's two seasons with F2 machinery. With cash-strapped Alfa Romeo gone, and the unreliable British BRM team a last-minute withdrawal, Ferrari filled the top six positions.

KEY PERSON

Former racing driver and Alfa Romeo competitions manager Enzo Ferrari was among motor racing's most consistently dominant forces after he set up under his own name in 1947.

They dip in and out to suit their own agendas, often infuriating other stake-holders as well as the fans, but car manufacturers have led the way since the earliest days of motor racing, whether by running their own in-house teams or supplying private customers. In the early 1950s, racing's governing body was given a sharp lesson in the importance of manufacturers in ensuring Formula 1's health.

Postwar shortages of raw materials meant racing in the late 1940s and early 1950s was a make-do-and-mend affair, featuring self-built cars assembled from foraged scraps or aging racers that had first seen action in the 1930s. The Alfa Romeos that dominated F1's first two seasons, 1950 and 1951, dated back to 1937, when Enzo Ferrari was running Alfa's competitions department. In the interim, he had set up on his own and now his former employer was in his sights.

But nobody else seemed able or willing to rise to the challenge properly, so in late 1951 the governing body hastily drew up a new set of rules—most significantly, reducing the size of naturally aspirated engines from 4.5 liters to 2.5—due to come in to effect in 1954. The idea was to allow plenty of time for interested parties to develop cars and engines for the new formula, but it also meant there was little point in committing design resources to the present one. Faced with sparse grids, race promoters forced the FIA to open the World Championship to Formula 2 cars in 1952–1953.

Fortunately, the dawn of the new formula in 1954 brought a wealth of manufacturer interest, and not only from Ferrari. Mercedes joined, and their works team set new standards of professionalism. Perhaps more significantly, though, Maserati pitched in as both a "works" team and as a supplier of private entries. The sweet-handling Maserati 250F was a mainstay of F1 grids for the following five seasons.

TAKING CARE OF BUSINESS
SPONSORS TAKE OVER

FUN FACT

Probably the longest-standing sponsor in F1 is the Shell fuel and lubes brand, which arrived as a Ferrari supplier in the second race of 1950.

HISTORICAL TIDBIT

In the late 1970s, the Hesketh and Surtees teams caused minor controversies by carrying logos from Penthouse magazine and the Durex condom brand.

KEY PERSON

Over the past decade, American businessman Zak Brown has been F1's biggest commercial mover and shaker, introducing major new sponsors to several teams. He was headhunted by McLaren to become their executive director at the end of 2016.

Watch any modern automobile race, from the club level on up, and you'll see cars bedecked in varying quantities of sponsor logos. For race fans, this is as unsurprising as the coming of the dawn each day.

Until the late 1960s, though, most teams raced in their national colors: blood red for Italy, deep blue for France, green for Britain, and so on. Sponsors' badges might be discreetly stitched onto a driver's overalls or displayed as banners around a team's pit, but on the cars? Unthinkable—and forbidden by the rules.

The turning point came in 1968, after a number of tire, fuel, and lubes suppliers ended the long-established practice of supplying their Formula 1 customers for free in exchange for . . . well, that was the problem. Without being able to explicitly connect their brand with the cars, there wasn't much return on their investment. Responding to the threat of dwindling sponsorship, the governing body grudgingly relaxed the rules on displaying logos.

Many people within the sporting firmament reacted with horror, especially when Lotus—then one of the leading teams—dropped their British racing green color scheme entirely, decking out their racing cars and their transporter in the red and gold of the Player's cigarette company. At a non-championship race at Brands Hatch in the UK that March, circuit authorities refused to let Lotus on track unless they blacked out the Player's logo on the side of their cars.

Part of the problem was that many race promoters were used to cutting their own deals for trackside advertising and event sponsorship, expecting a degree of exclusivity. But the tide could not be stopped. For teams, keeping up with the latest technology was an increasingly expensive business, and the most successful on track were those who embraced all the commercial opportunities that came their way.

TAKING CARE OF BUSINESS
ECCLESTONE'S REBELLION

FUN FACT

For many years there were rumors that Ecclestone had been involved in the Great Train Robbery of 1963. Asked about this in a newspaper interview, he remarked, "There wasn't enough money on that train. I could have done something better."

HISTORICAL TIDBIT

Ecclestone bought the assets of the defunct Connaught F1 team in 1958 and even drove laps in practice for two Grands Prix. His performance was described sniffily by one magazine as "not a serious attempt."

KEY PERSON

Frenchman Jean-Marie Balestre was the president of the FIA during the 1980s and an almost implacable enemy of Ecclestone. But his pomposity was a weakness in negotiations.

No look at Formula 1 history is complete without the man who shaped its fortunes for the better part of forty years. Bernie Ecclestone was a sharp-eyed motorcycle and automobile dealer from London who got involved in motor racing through 500cc-engined Formula 3 in the early 1950s, later graduating to driver management and team ownership.

A consummate wheeler-dealer, Ecclestone was said to be able to value an entire showroom of cars at a glance. Having bought the Brabham team in 1972, he spotted a much greater business opportunity.

When Ecclestone got involved, teams were still having to bargain individually with race promoters for their fees (known as "start money"), generally based on their box office potential. During the 1970s, Ecclestone in effect unionized the teams, pulling them together as a collective-bargaining force. Many of the team owners viewed themselves as gentlemen and racers first, feeling that the grubby matters of commerce were beneath them; they were happy to let Ecclestone do the legwork in exchange for a cut.

Since the race promoters were usually bigwigs from auto clubs that formed the membership of the FIA, this put Ecclestone into opposition against the FIA itself. Still, he and his legal expert, Max Mosley, managed to play hardball. By 1981, they went toe-to-toe with the FIA and threatened a breakaway series if they didn't get a fair cut of the money *and* a say in the rules.

The truth was that Ecclestone's Formula 1 Constructors' Association (FOCA) didn't have the resources to arrange a breakaway series. They were almost out of money. But the FIA could only count on the backing of two or three manufacturer-backed teams (one of which, Ferrari, delighted in playing both sides off against one another). As both sides stepped back from mutually assured destruction, Ecclestone largely got what he wanted.

TAKING CARE OF BUSINESS
A GLOBAL SPORT

FUN FACT

The US Grand Prix in Austin, Texas, is one of F1's most-watched races—96.1 million people worldwide tuned to the live broadcast of the 2015 event.

HISTORICAL TIDBIT

Newsreel footage of earlier racing events exists, but the 1953 British Grand Prix was the first F1 event to be broadcast live. The commentary was provided by Raymond Baxter, a former fighter pilot who had flown Spitfires in World War II.

KEY PERSON

James Hunt was a pivotal figure in English-language TV broadcasting. His on-track rivalry with Niki Lauda in 1976 was the catalyst for the BBC deciding to screen the championship in full. After he became a commentator, his forthright style made for compelling viewing.

Television was the key to unlocking mega-revenues and expanding Formula 1 from what had been a mostly European sport into one that properly straddled the globe. But this was not properly understood until the late 1970s, when Bernie Ecclestone—whether by happy accident or farsightedness—began to pull in TV rights deals as part of his drive to expand his influence.

Before then, the prevailing view of many—particularly race promoters—was that screening a race on television would harm ticket sales, and therefore best avoided unless the broadcaster came bearing a pot of gold. Self-interest blinded them to the potential of growing the overall audience.

Broadcasters, on the other hand, were most likely to be interested in screening an event based in their territory—but were in no rush to commit themselves to screening "foreign" races or a full championship, particularly for a niche interest such as motor racing. This, remember, was a time when satellite technology was in a state of relative infancy. Transmitting sports footage long-distance was costly and difficult, and most territories had just a handful of TV channels, many of which didn't broadcast 24/7.

But all that changed during the 1980s and 1990s as satellite technology forged ahead. As the number of channels grew, so too did the competition between them. The rights to transmit live sports became a key area of conflict and Ecclestone, having parceled up the F1 TV rights cheaply at a time when most people thought they had no value, was well placed to take advantage.

In the early 1980s, Ecclestone had to strong-arm broadcasters into screening all the races; by the late 1990s, they were desperate to pay him ever greater sums for the privilege. Formula 1 was one of the biggest sports in the world, commanding huge viewing figures. Governments in countries such as Malaysia, China, Korea, and India were falling over themselves to build lavish new circuits and get involved.

TAKING CARE OF BUSINESS
WHO ARE THESE PEOPLE?

FUN FACT

EM.TV, the media corporation that bought 50 percent of F1's commercial rights holder at the height of the dotcom boom in 2000, also owned Muppet makers The Jim Henson Company.

HISTORICAL TIDBIT

In a 2009 newspaper interview, Ecclestone courted controversy by describing Adolf Hitler as the kind of man who was "able to get things done."

KEY PERSON

Donald Mackenzie, head of CVC Capital Partners, held notional control of F1's commercial rights for ten years but was rarely seen in the paddock. He preferred to let Ecclestone remain the face of the business.

As the wealth generated by Formula 1's emergence as a global sport increased in magnitude, so too did the arguments over who should share in it. The result were year-on-year battles for control and ownership of the sport.

In the early days of Bernie Ecclestone's "rule," team owners were mostly happy to let him do the commercial hard work in exchange for a cut of the proceeds. Fast forward a decade or more and much had changed. First, having got out of the team ownership game (he sold Brabham in 1989), Ecclestone had turned his attention fully to the business of F1.

Teams, for their part, had become more corporate, as car manufacturers and other large companies sought a piece of the action and bought in. The days of teams being run by the person whose name was above the door were over.

A turning point came when Ecclestone tried to float his holding company, which owned the commercial rights to the sport, on the stock exchange in 1997. Only then did the teams properly grasp the extent to which F1's "ringmaster" had opened up new revenue streams (such as from trackside signage and hospitality) and concealed them from scrutiny via offshore companies. Even the accountancy firm doing due diligence for the flotation struggled to pin down what was going where.

The float did not happen, and a health scare prompted Ecclestone to transfer ownership of the commercial rights holding company to a family trust, based offshore, to benefit his wife and daughter in the event of his death. Ecclestone remained, but now as an employee. The trustees then sold significant holdings to a media company that almost immediately hit financial trouble. German media magnate Leo Kirch bought the assets, then went bust, leaving a trio of banks holding the rights. Then, in 2006, having been passed around like a tray of cakes, the rights were sold to a venture capitalist company, CVC Capital Partners.

TAKING CARE OF BUSINESS
F1 POST-ECCLESTONE

FUN FACT

CVC Capital Partners paid $1.7 billion for its F1 stake in 2006, selling it a decade later in a deal valuing it at $8 billion.

HISTORICAL TIDBIT

The commercial rights to F1 are actually leased from the FIA, albeit on generously long terms. Ecclestone secured a 100-year lease for $360 million in 2000 while the FIA was fighting an antitrust suit brought by the European Commission.

KEY PERSON

John Malone, the chairman of Liberty Media, is now among the most powerful media magnates in the world, with business interests that stretch from cable TV to live sports and music.

All venture capitalists like to cash out, sooner rather than later, so CVC Capital Partners' decade-long tenure as majority owner of Formula 1's commercial rights underlines how profitable the business is. Late in 2016, CVC agreed to sell to US giant Liberty Media. The clock was ticking on Bernie Ecclestone's reign.

Liberty immediately installed veteran US sports media executive Chase Carey, a longtime associate of Fox magnate Rupert Murdoch, as chairman, and an uncomfortable few months ensued as Ecclestone clung on to the levers of power. As soon as the deal went through in January 2017, Ecclestone was shunted into a non-executive "chairman emeritus" role and Carey assumed the top job.

No longer would F1 be run as a "one-man show," as Carey put it. Describing the sport's decision-making processes as "somewhere between ineffective and dysfunctional," Carey laid out a plan for a more conventional corporate management structure and a new focus on marketing the business. Ecclestone had been notably dismissive of digital media and increasingly short-term in his deal-making—largely because the leveraged nature of the CVC buyout made the sport hungry for cash.

To emphasize the new approach, Carey hired former ESPN vice president Sean Bratches to head up commercial operations, and the vastly experienced Ross Brawn—who had been both a technical director and a team principal in a forty-year F1 career—as sporting director. Bratches will be responsible for delivering Liberty Media's stated aim of increasing revenue by expanding the calendar, improving race promotion, engaging with the audience more widely and improving the spectator experience.

Brawn has the challenging mandate of rethinking the technical formula to deliver more on-track spectacle. This is likely to bring him into conflict with the FIA, which views the rules as its territory, and with the teams, who have been pressing for more influence on sporting as well as commercial matters. It's going to be a bumpy ride.

TIRE WARS

"Win on Sunday, sell on Monday" has long been the mantra of companies involved in motor racing, but the benefits of being involved in a global competition go beyond any marketing gains. Testing a product against its rivals creates opportunities to learn and innovate.

Everyday drivers all over the world now benefit from safer, better, more durable tires as a direct result of manufacturers battling with one another on the track. Sometimes, though, F1's tire wars got out of hand.

Until 1971, all F1 tires had a tread pattern, just like those of a road car. In the early years, teams would use the same tires in wet or dry conditions. This changed as Dunlop's R series of tires began to offer a variety of constructions, rubber compounds, and tread depths. Then, as Firestone and Goodyear arrived to break Dunlop's virtual monopoly in the late 1960s, the competition really took off.

Tires and wheels got wider and fatter, and the choices for teams and drivers to suit any given situation became still more baffling. Smooth-surfaced "slick" tires, introduced at the Spanish Grand Prix in 1971, promised better grip by having more rubber in contact with the surface—at a cost of being less able to disperse water when it rained.

Goodyear ruled through the mid-1970s, until Michelin arrived with the next big step-change, radial-belted tires, in 1977. These offered more outright grip than cross-plies, at a cost of a more abrupt breakaway once those limits were breached.

The downside of having two or more tire manufacturers racing to out-develop each other was exposed at the farcical US Grand Prix of 2005, where only six cars started the race, owing to fears that Michelin's tires might not be able to withstand the Indianapolis circuit's rigors. For 2008, the FIA enforced a single-supplier rule. These days, the only battle is over who gets the contract.

GLOSSARY

BUDGET CAP

A controversial measure first mooted in 2007 but now back on the table under the Liberty Media regime, a budget cap would aim to prevent teams from out-spending one another in their bid for success on the track. Without a cap, the richest teams will always win and the poorest will struggle to compete. New sporting chief Ross Brawn's stated aim is to enable small but clever teams to reap the rewards of agility.

CCB

Constructors' Championship Bonus payments are another commercial area of argument. While the top ten teams are given a share of the commercial revenues according to their finishing positions in the constructors' championship, Ferrari, Mercedes, Red Bull, and McLaren receive additional payments, regardless of where they finish. This dates back to the Ecclestone era, when these teams negotiated the extra funds as a condition of committing to F1 until at least 2020.

CONCORDE AGREEMENT

The top-secret contract between the FIA, Formula One Management, and the teams, this agreement lays out how Formula 1's commercial revenues are divided. The first was signed in 1981, the most recent in 2013. It has often been a fiercely contested area of negotiation—the 1997 Agreement expired at the end of 2007 without a new one put in place until 2009.

ESCALATOR

Each circuit that hosts a Grand Prix pays a sanctioning fee (see below) to Formula One Group, the commercial rights holder. Typically, the contracts to host races include an "escalator clause" under which the amount paid increases 10 percent or more year-on-year.

FOCA

The Formula One Constructors' Association became a potent entity with Bernie Ecclestone and Max Mosley at its head during the 1970s and 1980s, in effect unionizing the teams as a collective bargaining force against race promoters. By the end of the 1980s, it had metamorphosed into Formula One Management (now the Formula One Group), which collected revenues and then passed the teams their share.

FOTA

The Formula One Teams Association was a short-lived body formed by the teams in 2008. For many years the teams had suspected that Bernie Ecclestone's Formula One Management was acting hand-in-glove with the FIA, whose president was Ecclestone's former associate, Max Mosley. They united to demand more of a voice in sporting and commercial matters; once Mosley stepped down in 2009, their unanimity dissipated and the organization collapsed.

GPWC

In 2001, BMW, FIAT, Ford, Mercedes, and Renault founded GPWC Holdings, a joint company that would run their proposed breakaway series, the Grand Prix World Championship. They were moved to do so by Bernie Ecclestone's transfer of the sport's commercial rights to a family trust and the subsequent sale to media organizations involved in subscription television services. The fear was that migrating F1 coverage from terrestrial TV would reduce their audience reach, and therefore the value of their investment.

PADDOCK CLUB

Hospitality has been a lucrative revenue stream for F1, although for many years those sums remained hidden from view because the rights to run the luxurious and exclusive on-site "Paddock Club" facilities were leased to a Swiss company, Allsport Management.

RRA

The Resource Restriction Agreement was an idea proposed by FOTA, similar to the concept of a budget cap. Under its terms, the teams would reduce their factory head counts as well as the number of personnel travelling to races, while spending less on research and development. Only a few members stuck to it, and those that did soon had to reverse course.

SANCTIONING FEE

The payment for the right to host a Grand Prix, this fee is usually agreed upon by the race promoter and the commercial rights holder.

INDEX